Zermatt

A Mad Dog Ski resort guide

First edition 2007
Published by Mad Dog Ski
maddogski.com

Mad Dog Ski
Zermatt
First edition 2007

Published by Mad Dog Ski
Maps © Mad Dog Ski

Design: David Marshall
Printed by: Leycol
Edited by: Gaby de Pace

ISBN 0-9551215-6-6
ISBN 978-0-9551215-6-2

A catalogue record of this book is available at the British Library.

Mad Dog Ski, PO Box 6321, Bournemouth, BH1 9ED, UK
info@maddogski.com
maddogski.com
+44 (0) 845 054 2906

Contents

About Mad Dog Ski

About Zermatt

Planning your trip

On the piste

About Mad Dog guide books; why we write them and how they'll make a real difference to your holiday.

About Mad Dog Ski

Not so long ago, my time in the mountains was restricted to one or two precious weeks each winter. I would arrive in resort with my ski buddies, eager to get on the slopes as soon as possible and make the most of every minute there. I won't deny that, as well as wanting to make the most of time on piste, we all partied pretty hard and finding good après-ski spots and somewhere decent to re-fuel at lunchtimes played an important part of the holiday experience.

During my first season as a thirty-something chalet host, I realised I wasn't alone in my quest for reliable information. Week after week guests would ask the same questions; where should they ski, where were the best places to eat and drink, the best mountain restaurant? Mad Dog Ski was born.

Importantly, the information in Mad Dog guide books and on our website **maddogski.com** is written by skiers and boarders who actually live and work in the resort about which they are writing. Not only do they know the resort inside out, but they are passionate about helping you get the most out of your holiday from the moment you arrive to the moment you leave. We want you to love the resort and the mountains as much as we do.

With Mad Dog Ski, you can be confident that we will always give you our independent view; sometimes our taste may vary from yours but we only recommend our favourites. Extra special places and people are shown throughout this book as a 'Mad Dog favourites'. If you find places we haven't, or have a different view to ours, please write to us or email us at **info@maddogski.com**.

Enjoy the mountain!

Kate Whittaker
Founder, Mad Dog Ski

How to use this book

Mad Dog books are designed to be used in resort. To keep them small enough to fit in your jacket pocket, you'll find just the essentials you need to know in resort. For the full low down on planning your trip (your travel options, where to stay and other important stuff) check out the Planning your trip sections on **maddogski.com**.

The book has seven chapters:

About Zermatt

An introduction to the resort and the Zermatt ski area.

Planning your trip

Useful information to help you plan your holiday, including how to get to Zermatt and where to stay.

This is just a brief overview but see **maddogski.com** for more information than you ever knew you needed.

On the piste

Everything you need to get on the mountain as quickly as possible and to make the most of it when you get there. Includes an overview of the ski area, suggested day trips (including recommended lunch stops) as well as our unique piste ranking. You'll also find practical information about lift passes, ski schools and equipment hire.

Food and drink

Independent reviews of our favourite restaurants, bars and nightclubs. We've also visited all the mountain restaurants in the Zermatt ski area so you can make the most out of every mealtime.

Other things to do

Can't ski, won't ski – or just don't fancy it? This chapter contains everything that doesn't involve skiing or boarding. From high-adrenaline paragliding to blissful spas.

Children

Useful information for families, including our 'first day at ski school' checklist and our favourite family-friendly restaurants.

The list

Everything else! An A-Z of practical services and resort facilities including banks, buses, doctors and dentists.

Entries

Whilst every effort has been made to ensure that the contents of this book are accurate, places, prices and opening times change from season to season in ski resorts. If you spot an error or simply have a different opinion to us, please let us know at **info@maddogski.com**.

Signs and symbols

A key for the symbols used throughout the book is included at the beginning of the relevant section.

Maps

The map on page 9 shows the main landmarks we use to guide you about the resort.

Restaurants and bars are shown on page 82 and mountain restaurants are shown on page 102-3.

Prices

All prices are based on the 2005/6 season. Prices for food, drink and services in resort are given in Swiss francs (chf).

Skier or boarder?

Throughout this book, 'skiing' and 'skier' are used as interchangeable terms for 'riding' and 'boarder'. No offence is intended – it just seemed easier that way.

Telephone numbers

All numbers are prefixed by their international dialling code. You can tell a landline number in Zermatt as it begins (after the international code): 027 while Swiss mobile numbers start with '07'. The German word for mobile phone is 'Handy'.

The international dialling code from the UK to Switzerland is '00 41'. Do not dial the first '0' of the Swiss number. From Switzerland to the UK, dial '00 44' and omit the first '0' of the UK area code.

Although mobiles are as ubiquitous in Zermatt as the UK, you will find public telephones throughout the resort. Amongst other places, you will find them by the train station and in the post office. To use them, you will need to buy a phone card from a kiosk or use your credit card.

If you plan to use your UK mobile, check with your network provider that it is activated for international calls before leaving the UK. You pay to receive calls as well as make them, so text messages are a popular way to stay in touch on the mountain.

Resort updates and weather reports

maddogski.com has snow reports, webcams and weekly reports from our Zermatt-based researchers. You can also sign up for our regular newsletter at **maddogski.com/newsletter.html.**

About our researchers

Erica Meredith Hardy

After completing her degree, Erica worked a stint in the City but traded the rat race for a life in the mountains where she is now also a director of Summit Ski and Snowboard School. She has lived in Zermatt for five years, is a BASI instructor and is sponsored by Rossignol.

Favourite piste: Obere National (black – 8)
Favourite restaurant: Rua Thai
Best après-ski: The Hënnu Stall
Top mountain restaurants: Marmottes

Henry Meredith Hardy

Originally from London, Henry has now lived in Zermatt for six years and is a director of Summit Ski and Snowboard School. A fully qualified ski instructor (BASI 1), and telemark instructor, he has previously taught in Verbier and New Zealand. As well as instructing, Henry is also a mountain photographer (www.skiingsomewhere.com) and took the great covershot.

Favourite piste: Furgg-Furi (black – 62)
Favourite restaurant: The Pipe
Best après-ski: The Papperla Pub
Top mountain restaurant: Findlerhof

Tell us what you think!

You can give feedback on your favourite (or least favourite!) places in Zermatt at maddogski.com. Simply check the entry under our 'Mad Dog listings' section and click on 'Write review' or 'Rating'.

We'd love to hear from you; you can contact us by email, post or through our website. Full details are at the front of the book. If you write to us with comments on Zermatt, we will add them to our website and include your name in the next edition of this guide. If you don't want your comments reproduced, or your name mentioned, please say so.

Zermatt; the inside view of what makes it such an unforgettable resort.

Sitting beneath the most recognisable of Switzerland's peaks, the Matterhorn, Zermatt is rightly numbered amongst the top ski resorts in the world. Perhaps this is down to the stunning location, at 1620m in the beautiful Valais region of Switzerland.

Zermatt's ski area consists of over 300km of marked slopes, 38km of unpisted downhill routes and some of the most breathtaking off-piste you'll find in the Alps. If you enjoy food, the abundant choice of excellent mountain restaurants and the many different cuisines to be found down in the charming town will make your holiday. Whichever of these is most important to you, it's easy to see why Zermatt deserves its reputation as a world-class resort.

Zermatt at a glance

- 5,550 residents
- Around 15,000 beds to fill
- Tourists from the world over including Japan and USA
- 313kms of pisted slopes across the Matterhorn Ski Paradise
- 21% of pisted blue runs, 58% red, 21% black
- 69kms of snow-making equipment
- The Matterhorn (4478m) is one of the most famous and recognisable peaks in the Alps
- The Zermatt Ski Paradise spans two countries: Switzerland and Italy
- A member of the 'Best of the Alps' resorts

Orientation: Zermatt's main landmarks and areas

- **Bahnhofstrasse:** the main street that runs through the centre of town from the station
- **Bahnhofplatz:** the square next to the train station
- **Hofmattstrasse:** another central street; turn right out of the train station, walk 100m up Bahnhofstrasse and turn left
- **Kirchstrasse:** the street that runs down beside the church and over the river
- **Mattervispa river:** flows along though the middle of town from south to north
- **Gornergrat Bahn:** the rack-and-pinion railway located opposite the main train station
- **Sunnegga Express lift station:** down on the river at the north-eastern end of town
- **Klein Matterhorn lift station:** at the southern end of town at the end of the green bus route
- **Tourist office:** next to the train station in the square
- **Alpine Centre:** halfway up the main street, opposite the Mont Cervin Palace hotel
- **Church:** hard to miss; in the middle of Zermatt on the main street

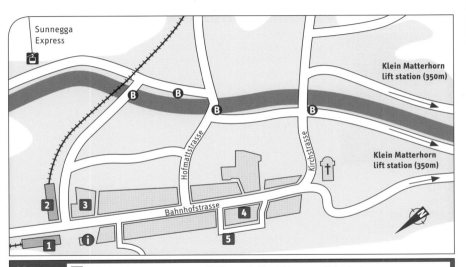

Sunnegga
Express

Klein Matterhorn
lift station (350m)

Klein Matterhorn
lift station (350m)

Hofmattstrasse

Kirchstrasse

Bahnhofstrasse

Key:

- Main shopping area
- ℹ Tourist office
- Ⓑ Bus stop

1. Matterhorn Gotthard Bahn
2. Gornergrat Bahn
3. Shopping centre

4. Alpine Centre
5. Post office

The Matterhorn and Edward Whymper

Edward. Whymper. 1840 · 1911

The Matterhorn is one of the most famous mountains in the Alps and certainly one of the most photographed. The British have a long and successful history ingrained in Zermatt's past. It was, after all, an Englishman who led the first group to the summit of the Matterhorn.

Since 1857 there had been 19 failed attempts to reach the summit. In mid-July of 1865, Edward Whymper and a group of fellow countrymen and local guides set out from the Monte Rosa hotel in Zermatt to try again. At the same time another group were attempting the ascent from the Italian side. After a long and treacherous climb, Whymper's group managed to scale the 4478m mountain to the very top, beating the other group by just 250m. However, the groundbreaking success of 14 July 1865 is in the history books as much for its tragedy as its triumph. Whymper and his men stayed at the summit for an hour before attempting the tricky descent. On the way back down, one of the men slipped, taking with him three others who were attached to him by a rope. The rope snapped leaving behind Whymper and two local guides. The incident has been shrouded in controversy ever since as to whether the rope broke or was cut by one of the survivors to save the rest of the group.

You can see the rope itself as well as other memorabilia and photos in the new Alpine Museum (page 131), next to the church. The small graveyard adjacent to the church is reserved exclusively for the unlucky climbers who have perished trying to climb the surrounding peaks as well as others who have since lost their lives in that fateful expedition.

The town

If you travel to Zermatt by car or bus, you will have to leave it in the small village of Täsch and say goodbye to your fossil-fuelled vehicle and board a train which winds its way through the mountains to your destination. The town of Zermatt is car-free, adding to its mountain charm. On arrival at the station (*Bahnhof*) in town, the first things you'll notice are the sharp mountain air, a fleet of electric taxis ('*electros*') and even the odd horse-drawn carriage or sleigh. Visitors and locals alike travel around town by foot, in electric buses and taxis, or by bicycle. Although the high street is taxi free between 4pm and 7pm, outside of that time, the electros can come up behind you before

you hear the bell and they can cause quite a shock.

With no car to rely on, Zermatt can, at first, seem huge but the town is easy to navigate, with the main street (*Bahnhofstrasse*) running parallel to the river and the Matterhorn dominating the landscape at the southern end of town. The distinctive peak quickly becomes part of your holiday, as you spend time ambling up and down the main street checking out the upmarket jewellery shops dotted between sports outlets and ski schools. In fact, the steep slopes around the village leave you in no doubt that you're in a pedigree ski resort.

Surrounding the centre are a number of suburbs that you will probably only visit if you are staying there. Wiesti and Oberhäusern on the other side of the river are mainly residential with hotels such as the Christiania and the Parkhotel Beau-Site as well as numerous chalets and private residences. Oberdorf and Am Bach, towards the Matterhorn end of town still have buildings from the original farming village of Zermatt. And at the southern end of town, you'll find the outlying suburb of Winkelmatten, a picturesque area next to the Klein Matterhorn lift station. If you keep walking along the river past the Klein Matterhorn lift station, you can follow the paths up to the sleepy hamlet of Furi, home to some charming mountain restaurants.

Zermatt has been offering accommodation to its summer and winter visitors for over 150 years, and with around 116 hotels and 1800 holiday apartments you will certainly find something to suit both your style and budget. You can choose from hostels, 2-star hotels and basic apartments if you are looking to keep costs to a minimum. But, if you want to live it up a little, Zermatt can offer you some of the most luxurious hotels and apartments in the world. With a good mid-range choice too, you should be able to find just the right place to stay to make your visit perfect.

As well as all the options in town, you can also stay on the mountain itself. The 100-year-old Hotel Kulm Gornergrat re-opened in 2006 and, at the top of the Gornergrat rack-and-pinion railway line, it is the highest hotel in the Alps (3100m). The Riffelalp Resort Hotel, found lower down on the Gornergrat train line, is a spectacular 5-star resort sitting in the forest above Zermatt. You can also stay in Furi at the Hotel Silvana, or even on the hillside, overlooking the town at the newly opened chic Omnia hotel.

For full details on travel to Zermatt and accommodation when you arrive, check out **maddogski.com**.

Heinz Julen

It is difficult to walk around Zermatt and not see the work of the town's most prolific artist, designer and architect. Born in 1964, into one of the main families in Zermatt, and named after Mr Heinz (think ketchup), Julen studied at art school in nearby Sion before realising he couldn't live without the mountains. Returning to his home, he set up a mountain studio and began projects that would give him national and international fame.

Vernissage – A cinema, art gallery and bar that was built on the ashes of the family home. A spiral staircase takes you from street level down to a dark wood loft-style bar with exposed girders and leather sofas. This is the perfect place to relax with friends over a cocktail, whilst the integral cinema provides daily showings. Visitors can also browse the art gallery with works by both Julen himself and other artists. *www.vernissage-zermatt.com*

Viewhouse – four stylised apartments within a house, built from scratch by Julen in 1993, with uninterrupted views of the Matterhorn. *www.viewhouse.ch*

Into the Hotel – A project that ended in a controversy that is still sensitive in Zermatt today, *Into the Hotel* opened in 2000 as a chic top class hideaway aimed at the jet set. This elaborately designed hotel had unique characteristics that drew customers from all over the world. Unfortunately, problems between the investors and the designer forced the hotel to close just seven weeks after its inauguration and Julen's interior was ripped out. After sitting as an empty shell for six years, the hotel has just reopened as The Omnia. *www.heinzjulen.com, www.theomnia.com*.

The skiing

Offering some of the highest pistes in Europe, Zermatt's location means reliable snow and top skiing.

The high altitude and abundance of snow-making facilities mean that the season in Zermatt usually begins in the middle of November and lasts right through to May, making it one of the longest winter seasons in the Alps. In fact, with the large glacier at Klein Matterhorn it is possible to enjoy a turn or two all year-round.

Zermatt's ski area is divided into three: Sunnegga, Gornergrat and Klein Matterhorn; the latter also giving access to the Breuil-Cervinia ski area in Italy. But not everything is perfect – Zermatt is not a ski-in, ski-out resort by any measure, and has just three lift stations to take you up the mountain (page 26). However, to balance this, neither is it a purpose-built monstrosity. What it lacks in easy access to the mountain is more than made up for by the picturesque Swiss Alpine town, the range of the ski area and the seemingly unlimited number of tempting mountain restaurants.

The skiing has something for everyone although it hasn't always been an obvious choice for beginners. However, with recent improvements in the lift system and the addition of many new ski schools in the past few years, this is no longer the case. For the intermediate skier the selection of pistes on which to progress is endless and for the advanced skier there is a challenging selection of black runs and unpisted downhill runs (marked on your piste map in yellow), many of which end up with some of the largest moguls in the Alps later on in the winter season.

Snowbaorders may find the seemingly endless flat paths and moguls frustrating but there are plenty of long jibbing runs and the off-piste is phenomenal.

Live life in luxury...

- Book a helicopter transfer from your airport to resort with Air Zermatt – page 129
- Stay in style and above the rest at the newly renovated Omnia hotel – page 20
- Eat dinner at the exclusive Mont Cervin Palace Grill – page 87
- Seek out the perfect piece at the Bucherer jewellery shop – page 140
- Pamper yourself at the newly opened Mirabeau wellbeing spa – page 127

The Zermatt lift pass may seem expensive (379chf for six days) but children under nine go free, under 16s pay half-price and the lift pass also covers your use of the electric buses in town. The lift system is state of the art; long gone are the chairlifts that hit you in the back of the calves, they've been replaced by high speed chairs with pull-down covers and comfortable seats.

For more details of the slopes awaiting you, turn to **On the piste** (page 23) for an overview of the different areas and some fantastic recommended day trips designed to make exploring easier. We also include all the information you need to get on the mountain as quickly as possible.

Don't leave Zermatt without...

- Drinking in the surreal but fun bar of the Alex Hotel, a very welcoming and entertaining evening – page 95
- Eating at Le Mazot restaurant for a gourmet treat – page 86
- Skiing the cruisy 14km from the border down to Breuil-Cervina, Italy in one go – page 30
- Jumping around to bands at the Hënnu Stall after a hard day's skiing – page 96
- Scaring yourself on the heavenly (or hellish) Trifjti moguls – page 50
- Taking a glacier helicopter flight for the ultimate mountain view – page 33
- Getting away from it all and staying in a turret room at the Kulm Gornergrat hotel (3100m) – page 20
- Getting into the late night vibe at the trendy Vernissage – page 99
- Shaking your stuff at the Schneewittchen (under the Papperla Pub) – page 98
- Indulging in a traditional Swiss meal at the Whymper-stube (under the Hotel Monte Rosa) – page 91

Helping you to
plan your trip,
with information on
how to get to Zermatt
and where to stay.

What you'll find in this chapter...

In this chapter you'll find a useful overview to help you plan your holiday including how to get to Zermatt and where to stay when you get there.

Our books are designed to be most useful in resort and so this chapter carries only the bare essentials you need to plan your trip. Use **maddogski.com** for all the latest information and more detail.

Check out **maddogski.com**:
- A full range of travel options to Zermatt as well as contact details for travel companies, helpful advice on travelling and up-to-date flight routes
- Accommodation advice including reviews and contact details for a range of places to stay
- A listings facility allowing you to narrow your search down and find the information you need quickly
- Advice on all aspects of booking your trip from insurance to the latest snow reports straight from resort

Getting there

Geneva is the closest and most convenient airport to get to Zermatt – with regular flights from all over the UK.

Geneva airport is 217km from Zermatt which means just under three hours in a car to Täsch (and then a short train ride) or a four hour train journey to Zermatt itself.

You can hire a car at the airport (remember to ask for snow chains) to drive as far as Täsch, where you have to park the car (page 154) and take the scenic Matterhorn Gotthard Bahn which winds up through the narrow valleys all the way to the car-free resort. The train runs frequently and takes just 12 minutes to reach Zermatt. It costs around 15chf for a return ticket.

If you prefer to sit back and take in the scenery, the Swiss rail system is one of the most efficient and punctual in the world.

Airport transfer times

Airport	Kilometres to Zermatt	Approximate transfer time time by road	Approximate transfer time by train (changes)
Sion	74km	1 hour 30 minutes	2 hours (1)
Geneva	217km	2 hours 40 minutes	4 hours (1)
Zurich	240km	3 hours 30 minutes	5 hours (1 or 2)
Milan (Malpensa)	244km	3 hours 30 minutes	4 hours (1 or 2)
Basel	250km	3 hours 15 minutes	5 hours (2 or 3)

Get onto a train at Geneva airport and, apart from one easy change, you can relax and enjoy the ride.

Although more expensive, it is possible to get taxis from the airport or private transfers from companies such as Ski Hoppa or Go routair (page 22).

You can also fly to Zurich, Basel and Milan, though all have slightly longer transfer times. And if it's a local airport you're after, fly to Sion (just 74km from Zermatt) with a charter flight on Saturdays from London Gatwick when you book with Ski Flights. Or fly business-class with Zermatt's local airline Alpwings (from London City or Gatwick) although this service only runs over the weekends.

Where to stay

As you'd expect, Zermatt's mainstay of accommodation options consists of luxurious hotels and top-end chalets and it's hard to wander the streets without seeing some of this affluence. That said, visitors' expectations are high here, so 2, 3 and 4-star chalets and hotels tend to provide more value for money than in other ski resorts. And with low-priced hotels and self-catering apartments readily available, those on a budget will find a good range of options.

Tour operators and holiday companies book properties across the price range and in various locations so they can be a wise option for hassle-free planning. For more information and contact details, see **maddogski.com**.

If you prefer to cook your own meals or eat out, then try a self-catered apartment from companies such as Zermatt Holidays (www.zermattholidays.com). Or if you're looking for something different, book yourself into one of the four state-of-the-art apartments in View House – designed by local artist and architect, Heinz Julen (page 13).

For a chalet experience where all you have to worry about is putting your boots on in the morning, Mountain Exposure (www.mountainexposure.com) offer luxury catered chalets of varying sizes.

The one aspect of Zermatt's accommodation that rises well above the rest are their hotels – of which

there are many. In Zermatt, you can stay at the highest hotel in the Alps, the 3-star Kulm Gornergrat. This hotel sits at 3100m, at the top of the Gornergrat railway, providing its guests with the most spectacular sunsets and sunrises. There is also the newly opened, very chic Omnia hotel which sits majestically just above the town. Or for a warm welcome and a lively atmosphere, the 4-star Hotel Alex is a big favourite with the Brits. If you want a truly unforgettable experience, spend a night in your own igloo in the Igloo Village (page 130). Lastly, if it is old-fashioned luxury you are after, the formal 5-star Mont Cervin Hotel is hard to miss with its huge entrance dominating the main street.

For more details, reviews and contact information, check out **maddogski.com**

Useful numbers and websites

Airports
Geneva airport:
W: www.gva.ch,
T: +41 (0)22 717 71 11

Zurich:
W: www.zurich-airport.com
T: +41 (0)43 816 2211

Basel:
W: www.euroairport.com
T: +41 (0)61 325 3111

Milan:
W: www.sea-aeroportimilano.it
T: +39 02 74852200

Sion:
W: www.sionairport.ch
T: +41 (0)27 329 0600

Airlines
Alpwings:
W: www.alpwings.ipeak.ch
T: +41 (0)27 967 66 83

British Airways:
W: www.ba.com
T: +44 (0)870 850 9850

easyjet:
W: www.easyjet.com
T: +44 (0)905 821 0905

Flybe:
W: www.flybe.com
T: +44 (0)871 522 6100

Ski Flights:
W: www.ski-flights.com
T: +44 (0)870 830 8136

Swiss:
W: www.swiss.com
T: +44 (0)845 601 0956

Trains
Swiss Rail:
W: www.sbb.ch

Matterhorn Gotthard Bahn:
W: www.mgbahn.ch,
T: +41 (0)27 927 7777

Car hire
Alamo:
W: www.alamo.co.uk
T: +44 (0)870 400 4562

Avis:
W: www.avis.co.uk
T: +44 (0)844 581 0147 (Sion)

Budget:
W: www.budget.co.uk
T: +44 (0)844 581 2231
(not Basel)

easycar:
W: www.easycar.co.uk
T: +44 (0)8710 500 444

Europcar:
W: www.europcar.co.uk
T: +44 (0)845 758 5375 (Sion)

Hertz:
W: www.hertz.co.uk
T: +44 (0)870 844 8844 (Sion)

Private transfers

Alpine Cab:
W: www.alpinecab.com

Alp Line:
W: www.alp-line.com
T: +33 (0)4 50 74 38 42

ATS:
W: www.a-t-s.net
T: +44 (0)709 209 7392

Go Routair:
W: www.goroutair.ch
T +41 (0)29 422 29 85

Ski Hoppa:
W: http://ski.resorthoppa.com
T: +44 (0)871 855 1101

Self-drive advice

RAC Route Planner:
W: www.rac.co.uk

Driving abroad advice:
W: www.drivingabroad.co.uk

Insurance

Insure and go:
W: www.insureandgo.com
T: +44 (0)870 901 3674

Ski Club of GB:
W: www.skiclub.co.uk
T: +44 (0)845 601 94227

Ski Insurance:
W: www.ski-insurance.co.uk
T: +44 (0)870 755 6101

It is important to check with your insurance company what skiing activities they will cover. For instance, some companies regard Zermatt's downhill runs (yellow pistes) as off-piste.

You can also buy an Air Zermatt card for 30chf (valid for a year throughout Switzerland) at any Zermatt lift pass office to cover rescue costs including helicopter rescue or any transport needed.

Tourist office

Zermatt tourist office:
W: www.zermatt.ch
T: +41 (0)27 966 8100

This chapter gets you **on the piste** and around the mountain as quickly as possible — after all, it's why you're here.

What you'll find in this chapter...

The ski area

The lift system has seen a huge investment in the last few years, with three new lifts due to be completed by 2008. A new 8-man cable car to connect Furi and Riffelberg has opened this season, allowing a route from the Klein Matterhorn to Gornergrat sector.

With one of the highest lift pass prices in Europe, Zermatt offers 313km of pistes to explore between Italy and the Zermatt ski area enough to keep even the

Zermatt's vast ski area is called, rather grandly, the Matterhorn Ski Paradise and is made up of three different sectors: Sunnegga, Gornergrat, and Klein Matterhorn. From Klein Matterhorn you will find easy access into Breuil-Cervinia and Valtournenche in Italy.

fastest skiers busy all week! And with more than 50% of runs being glacial or serviced by snowmaking facilities, Zermatt can pretty much guarantee good snow conditions

throughout the season. If taking long lunches in the sun is your thing, there are also plenty of high-quality mountain restaurants (page 100) to choose from.

As the name suggests, the Sunnegga sector feels the heat of the sun, which in the colder winter months makes it popular with visitors and locals alike.

Sunnegga

The Sunnegga Express funicular takes just six minutes to deliver you to Sunnegga (though you may have to wait a little at the bottom). Here you are met with amazing views towards the Matterhorn, Gornergrat and Klein Matterhorn. As the name suggests, the Sunnegga sector feels the heat of the sun, which in the colder winter months makes it popular with visitors and locals alike.

On exiting the train you have four options with a range of runs to suit all levels. Firstly, you can continue up to the next main lift station, Blauherd, via Zermatt's new 'chondola' (a lift that alternates chairs and gondolas). Novices can walk down a tunnel to reach the beginner area (a magic carpet and a very easy blue run make this an ideal spot to learn). You can also ski from Sunnegga down to Findeln, a popular choice at lunchtime as this tiny hamlet is home to some of Zermatt's best mountain restaurants (Findlerhof, page 110 and Chez Vrony, page 109, are just two of these). Your final option is the long wide **Brunnjeschbord (4)**, which will bring you down to the Patrullarve chairlift. From here, you can take the chairlift up to Blauherd or head back down to the town via a fun après-ski stop called Olympia, home to a very large terrace with spectacular Matterhorn views (page 116).

Blauherd is the departure point for one of the best runs in Zermatt for advanced skiers, the **Obere National (8)** - a black run that rolls its way in steep pitches back to the Patrullarve chairlift. Blauherd also allows cable car access to Rothorn, the highest point on this part of the ski area, offering amazing views of the Monte Rosa. From here, there are several runs of varying difficulty and you can ski all the way back to the town via Blauherd and Sunnegga. You can also reach Gornergrat from the top of Rothorn.

On the way down, follow the long **Fluhalp (19)** run past the Fluhalp restaurant (worth a visit but be sure to book, page 111) to Gant. Hop into the cable car up to Hohtälli and take in the views over the huge expanse of glacier - a reminder of how small we are in this vast scenery. From the top of the Hohtälli cable car, you can ski back round to Gant on one of Zermatt's most famous runs, the **White Hare (28)**, to get back to Sunnegga, or you can explore Gornergrat.

At Hohtälli you can also take another cable car to Triftji (home to one of Europe's big mogul competitions, the Triftji Bump Bash). Triftji (33) is a long, challenging bump run that keeps even expert skiers entertained for days. Loops can be done on a rather old and steep T-bar, which may sound like a nightmare to some, but for those who love this area it's just the way it should be.

Gornergrat

If you don't want to ski the whole way from Sunnegga, catch the Gornergrat train (page 10). Over 100 years old, this classic cog railway winds up the mountain delivering spectacular scenery along the way. It does take around

Over 100 years old, this classic cog railway winds up the mountain delivering spectacular scenery along the way.

40 minutes to reach the top but the views are worth the wait. This winter, the trains are being replaced by faster twin entry-level railcars which will hopefully make for a more comfortable and streamlined service.

Once up on Gornergrat, a new high speed 6-man chairlift provides access to several rolling blue runs that have earned Gornergrat the title of intermediate's heaven.

Getting to the ski area

One of the problems you will face every day is how to get to the ski area. There are only three routes up to the main pistes and it is worth deciding where you want to ski and checking weather forecasts before you embark on your journey.

Unfortunately there will always be queues at peak holiday times especially between 9-10am when the ski schools start. Avoid the rush by getting up earlier or starting later. Also remember that lunchtime can be the quietest time of day for skiing.

Sunnegga

This underground train starts from next to the river (page 9) and whisks you up to the Sunnegga sector from 8.30am. Perfect when the weather is cold and windy, this area is more sheltered and gets more sun than any of the others. Sunnegga is also a good place to learn (page 33).

Gornergrat

Not the fastest choice but definitely a scenic one. This rack-and-pinion railway leaves from (page 10) every 20 minutes from 8am and will chug its way up to the top of the Gornergrat in around 40 minutes, allowing you to explore that sector. To speed things up a little, get out at Riffelberg and get chairlift 'M' up to the top.

Klein Matterhorn

Take the faster gondola from this station (page 10) from 8.30am up to Furi and the connecting lifts.

Once at Furi, if you are headed up to the Klein Matterhorn or Italy, head left to the cable car to Trockener Steg (the other takes you to Schwarzsee). At the top of this cable car, jump straight on the next one and you're on your way to the highest point of the ski area.

This station is also a common return point at the end of the day so be prepared to queue for buses or join the lines for taxi-sharing back into the centre.

Advanced skiers shouldn't be put off as there are more challenging runs too; from the top of the chair take a steep winding red run back down to Gant and the Sunnegga sector or access the challenging mogul runs at Triftji.

Heading down from the chairlift, a red run continues past Riffelalp (and its 5-star luxury resort hotel) and eventually down to Furi. Once you reach there, you can either choose to continue down to Zermatt or go up and ski the Klein Matterhorn domain.

Gornergrat is also popular with non-skiers; the train stops at several stations on the way up so it's easy to meet up with skiing friends for lunch or a drink. The many easy walking and snowshoeing paths

At 3883m above sea level, you have reached the highest ski area in Europe.

(page 133) and the dedicated toboggan run (page 135) attract skiers and non-skiers alike.

Klein Matterhorn

This is the largest most extensive ski area and accessed via the Matterhorn Express gondola which leaves from the end of town. Take the bus with the green bumper and stay on as far along the river as it goes; when you get off cross over the bridge and take the elevator which delivers you to the lift station. The gondola and cable car leave here to go to Furi from where you can either go on up to Schwarzsee

(where it feels like you can practically touch the Matterhorn) or get out and take the cable car to Trockener Steg and onto the Klein Matterhorn. Most people take the latter option, as it accesses some of the best skiing of the area and is also the way to head if you are going to Italy for the day.

Once at Trockener Steg, take another cable car to the top of Klein Matterhorn where you will feel the thinness of the air (you might find the altitude a bit disconcerting if you try it on your first day in the mountains or with a hangover – or both!). At 3883m

above sea level, you have reached the highest ski area in Europe. You can take an elevator even further up, to a viewing platform which enables you to see for miles around in all directions (the maps point out the peaks visible in Switzerland, Italy and France).

Zermatt offers skiing 365 days a year, and the glacier between Trockener Steg and the very top is open in the summer.

Skiing back down Klein Matterhorn, you'll find several wide red runs taking you toward Trockener Steg or you can head over the border into Italy and access the Breuil-Cervinia ski area (page 30). If you choose Trockener Steg you will find another new high-speed 6-man chairlift taking

you to three fantastic red runs, as well as a snowpark and half-pipe, should you wish to try a few jumps.

On the Swiss side it is fairly easy to find your way around; from the top, everything funnels down to Furgg where you can loop back up to Trockener Steg via chairlift or cable car or head up to Schwarzsee. The last option from here is the **Furgg-Furi (62)**, a black piste heading back towards town. This is a great run but best skied in the morning as it's one of the major routes off the mountain and can get very busy towards the end of the day.

Schwarzsee is on the far right of the Zermatt side of the piste map and offers awesome views from right under the north face of the Matterhorn. There is another great

Using the piste map

Free piste maps are available from the tourist office, ski schools and major lift stations.

Looking at the piste map, Sunnegga is on the left, Gornergrat in the middle and Klein Matterhorn on the right of the Swiss side.

Without doubt, the ski area is more suited for intermediate and advanced skiers than beginners, but those who have never skied before should head for the areas marked on the piste map with a blue 'L' which are positioned with the rest of the runs, rather than close to the town (page 33). Intermediate skiers will find endless terrain to keep them busy, and advanced skiers can take advantage of Zermatt's exciting black pistes and downhill ski routes (marked but unprepared pistes, usually steep and challenging mogul runs). Snowboarders will find the many paths and flat sections on the pisted terrain a bit of an annoyance, although there is a well-stocked snowpark up on the glacier with a decent-sized half-pipe (page 31). However with the amount of off-piste and glacier riding to be done, as well as heli-skiing, boarders should find plenty to keep them occupied.

Throughout the book, runs are coloured by their grading (blue, red etc) as well as a number that corresponds to a key of names in the top right-hand corner. When skiing, look out for signposts with the number and colour of the run. Breuil-Cervinia pistes show the colour and number of the piste but not the names.

Pistes are also marked with posts indicating the colour of the runs. Right-hand posts are marked with 1m of fluorescent paint and left-hand with 30cm of fluorescent paint, helping you find your way even in bad visibility.

run down to town, the **Weisse Perle (51)** which winds its way around the mountain and then down through the trees back to Furi. Here you will find the Hörnli T-bar which takes you toward the famous Hörnli Ridge, and has some exciting red and black runs from the top.

Skiing from either Furgg or Schwarzsee you pass through Furi, and its fantastic mountain restaurants (page 105). From Furi into town, you'll pass another of Zermatt's gourmet restaurants with rustic charm, Zum See (page 123) which is definitely one worth pre-booking. Continuing down, if it's the end of the day, you'll hear the Hënnu Stall (page 96) before you reach it - one of the liveliest après-ski spots on the mountain. From

here, just a short ski (with a long flat schuss at the end) will bring you home, where taxis and buses await to help you back to your accommodation. In peak times, there are often queues here but they move pretty quickly.

Breuil-Cervinia
The Zermatt International lift pass allows you to ski over to the Italian Breuil-Cervinia ski area. Strictly speaking, you should take your passport with you into Italy although, in practice, checks are rarely made. Most restaurants also accept Swiss francs.

Ski from the top of Klein Matterhorn across the border into Italy. The classic run is the **Ventina (7)**, around 14km of rolling red run

The classic run is the Ventina (7), around 14km of rolling red run all the way from the top down to the village.

all the way from the top down to the village. You'll find lots of junctions on the way down but they all end up in the same place so just enjoy the cruise down. Also part of this area is Valtournenche; usually much quieter and a secret gem during peak holiday weeks.

The Breuil-Cervinia ski area is a large bowl and on a clear day it's easy to navigate. Most runs are blues and cruisy reds, and are great for intermediate skiers and

snowboarders to play around on. The fantastic and well-priced homemade pasta and Italian wines are often enough to entice people over for the day. Keep an eye on the time though; if you miss the last lift and get stuck on the Italian side it is an expensive six hour taxi ride back to Zermatt. If this does happen to you, most people find it easier and cheaper to spend the night there, (if you can find a room).

Boarders

While Zermatt's pistes are more geared towards skiers, with what seems like endless small paths, flat sections and mogul fields, there are definitely plus points for snowboarders. If piste-riding is your thing, head to Sunnegga or alternatively over to the Breuil-Cervinia bowl for some long runs perfect for jibbing.

The snowpark (see below) is also a big attraction for freestylers with many boarding camps focusing their time here. The Breuil-Cervinia snowpark is also worth investigating.

However, the major attraction for boarders in Zermatt is the epic off-piste, which explains why Zermatt goes pretty big on heli-boarding (page 32).

Snowparks

The Gravity Park on the glacier above Trockener Steg has kickers, rails, wall ride, box, rainbow, and a good half-pipe. You'll need to either walk the park or do loops on the

In Zermatt you must take a professional guide with you to navigate the endless crevasses and seracs that make up the glacial terrain. That said, with a guide, the terrain is endless and you can spend your whole week just exploring.

Furggsattel chairlift (V). Summer sees another park higher up on the glacier.

Off-piste, backcountry and heli-skiing

Unlike many French resorts where you can just go off-piste, in Zermatt you must take a professional guide with you to navigate the endless crevasses (deep fissures in the glacier) and seracs (ice cliffs) that make up the glacial terrain. That said, with a guide, the terrain is endless and you can spend your whole week exploring it. Also, unlike French ski resorts where heli-skiing is illegal, Zermatt positively encourages it through Air Zermatt and the Alpine Centre. If you are content to just play off the sides of the pistes, Gornergrat area has plenty to offer although remember that this can still be just as dangerous as going off into the backcountry. It is also important to check whether your travel insurance covers you going off-piste.

Alpine Centre

Bahnhofstrasse 58, 8.30am-12pm, 3-7pm, halfway up the main street, +41 (0)27 966 24 60, www.zermatt.ch/alpincenter.
Zermatt's expansive glacial terrain makes the hiring of a guide imperative if you want to venture away from the pistes and only mountain guides are able to teach and guide off-piste. Most of them are based here.

The Alpine Centre also offers daily helicopter tours (weather dependent) up to the top of the Zermatt ski area with a guide to bring you down through the glacial terrain. From 315chf.

Air Zermatt
Spissstrasse 107, turn left out of the station (the main street is on the right) and head to the end of town (about 500m); Air Zermatt is on your left, +41 (0)27 966 8686, www.air-zermatt.ch.
Heli-skiing trips and glacier flights.

Beginner runs and children's areas
Beginner areas are marked on the piste map with an 'L'.

Sunnegga
When you arrive at the top, take the doors on the right (looking up the tunnel) which lead via the lower exit to the beginner slope. It's a small area with a very gentle slope, and a 'magic carpet' lift to get you back up the hill. Once you're ready to move off the beginner area you can progress onto the very easy blue next door.

Riffelberg
The Swiss Ski School has a large children's beginner area up at Riffelberg (page 148). The area is serviced by a couple of magic carpets, rope tows, foam obstacles and hoops for the kids to ski around.

Trockener Steg
Looking down the piste at the top of Trockener Steg you will see a large beginner area just past the Furgsattel (V) 6-man covered chair. You'll find a flat section at the bottom (ideal for putting on your skis for the first time) and a gentle sloping hill above it; there is a rope tow giving access up the hill. Once beginners have mastered this slope they can progress to the easy blue run accessed by the Gandegg T-bar (X1).

Cross-country (*Langlauf*)
For cross-country skiing head to Täsch's 12km of trails (for transport options, see page 162).

Lift passes
Lift passes in Zermatt are hands-free cards that automatically operate the turnstiles at the lift stations. It is best to put your lift pass in a secure left-hand pocket and leave it there all week.

Day passes are not automatic

so you will need to feed them into the machine each time you pass. The same applies if you have upgraded your Zermatt pass, to allow you to ski in Breuil-Cervinia for the day.

If you have booked through a tour operator or a hotel, chances are that they will organise your lift pass for you. However, if you are travelling independently you can book before you arrive. Go to www.matterhornparadise.ch and click on 'rates' on the left-hand menu.

A few general points to bear in mind:
- All prices for the standard plastic ski pass include a refundable charge of 5chf. To reclaim your deposit, simply return your card

to any of the bottom lift stations or the tourist office at the end of your trip
- Your ski pass covers Zermatt but you have the choice of buying an 'international' ski pass that covers Breuil-Cervinia. If you only want to venture into Italy on one or two days, you can buy add-ons to your ski pass for that day
- Children under nine ski free, and children between the age of nine and 16 pay half-price
- For discounted passes (eg for senior citizens, children or youth) or free passes (for under nines) you will have to provide official ID with a photo, eg a passport
- Passport photos are not needed as all lift pass offices have a camera at the counter

Lift pass offices
Lift pass offices are located in all three of the main lift stations in town and in the Alpine Centre on the main street (page 9). They are open when the lifts are operating.

Lost Passes
If you lose your pass, go to any ticket office with your receipt. Your old pass will be deactivated and you will be issued with a new one, although you will have to pay a further 5chf deposit for the replacement card.

Lift closing times
Opening and closing times are found on the piste map although times vary throughout the season so it is worth checking them at the lift stations. Individual lift closing

times are also shown at the bottom of each lift. Gornergrat train times are on the piste map.

Piste security & emergency numbers

In the case of an accident call piste security: +41 (0)27 967 0101.

You can also call the Swiss emergency number 144 (from a Swiss mobile or landline) or +41 (0)333 333 333 (from a UK mobile).

Remember to give the operator detailed information on the location of the accident and the number of casualties. If you have some idea of the injuries sustained then let them know that too.

Adult lift pass prices (high season): Zermatt pass

No of days	Adult Chf	Senior (64+)
Half day (from 12.15pm)	52	44
1	68	58
5	290	247
6	336	286
10	497	422
Season	1365	1160
Cervinia add-on	37chf/day	

For details of cheaper prices for older children and young adults, see Children, page 145.

Safety

Most accidents are caused by collisions; it is relatively easy for adult skiers to achieve speeds of over 50kph, even children can quite easily reach 45kph. Be aware of others and make sure you follow the piste rules (page 36).

Avalanche reports:
187 +41 (0)848 800 187)
www.slf.ch

Travelling at high speed is one of the great attractions of skiing but remember that it brings an element of danger.

Rules of the piste

1. **Respect** – do not endanger or prejudice the safety of others

2. **Control** – ski in control, adapting your speed and manner to ability, conditions and traffic. Give way to slower skiers

3. **Choice of route** – the uphill skier must choose his route so he does not endanger the skiers below

4. **Overtaking** – allowed left or right, above or below but always leave sufficient space for the overtaking skier

5. **Entering and starting a run** – look both up and down the piste before you head off

6. **Stopping on the piste** – avoid stopping at narrow or low visibility areas. Always stop at the edge of the piste rather than in the middle and make sure that you can be easily seen by approaching skiers

7. **Climbing** – if you have to walk up or down the piste, do so at the edge and ensure neither you nor your equipment are a danger to anyone else

8. **Signs and markings** – respect the information given about pistes and the weather

9. **Accidents** – if you witness an accident, you must give assistance, particularly by alerting piste security

10. **Identification** – if you are involved in or witness an accident, you must provide your identity to piste security if requested

The International Ski Federation (FIS) Code of Conduct

Avalanche!

Avalanche risk is an ever present fact in high mountain regions and while Zermatt does a lot to prevent them, the danger cannot be completely averted and, tragically, every year people do die on the mountain.

Remember that much of Zermatt's off-piste is glacial terrain which is covered in crevasses (deep fissures in the glacier) and seracs (ice cliffs). The icy nature of glaciers mean that many people slip into crevasses or off cliffs. You must ski with a professional guide who knows the Zermatt terrain if you want to venture onto glaciers.

Information is available at the bottom of every lift base in town on the present avalanche risk, with five lights:

1	Low
2	Moderate
3	Considerable
4	High
5	Very high

It is important to remember that this grading is all encompassing for the whole ski area and does not guarantee your safety – if you want information about a specific area, ask a ski patroller.

Speed is of the essence if you are caught in an avalanche; if the victim is still alive after the initial impact there is an 80% chance of survival if rescued in the first 12 minutes, after 15 minutes the probability of a successful rescue drops dramatically. Your best chance of survival is to be rescued by someone in your own group; a transceiver, shovel and probe are essential kit for off-piste skiing. Although manufacturers claim that mobile phones cause minimum interference with transceiver signals, it is also recommended that you switch off your mobile whilst off-piste.

Weather

The weather forecast is posted outside the tourist office every day and every morning, the Zermatt channel shows webcams from each of the areas as well as the temperature and wind strength. Take note of this as looks can be deceiving; even a bright windless sunny day in January can be a numbing -20°C!

There are information boards at the three lift stations in town showing open/closed pistes and lifts, along with temperature, wind, snow conditions and avalanche warnings.

Bad weather days

There will always be days where the winds are ripping around the mountains and the snow is doing

Take note of the weather forecast as looks can be deceiving; even a bright windless sunny day in January can be a numbing -20°C!

its best to blind you. At times like these, ski in places with as little exposure and as much shelter as possible such as lower slopes or those through the trees. Sunny spots such as the Blauherd to Sunnegga and Gornergrat can be good choices depending on the wind direction. Almost certainly though, on these days, the Klein Matterhorn will be closed as well as the slopes down to Breuil-Cervinia.

The tourist office publicises things to do on bad weather days under 'events' on their website: www.zermatt.ch. Alternatively, pop into the office itself about activities on offer or look at **Other things to do** (page 125).

Ski and snowboard schools

Zermatt has undergone some big changes in this area in the last five years. With Stoked initially breaking the monopoly of the Swiss school, others have followed. This means that, unusually for the Swiss Alps, there is now a huge choice of ski schools in Zermatt.

With all the schools it is important to book as early as possible for peak times. The prices we give here should be used as a guide – the websites give up-to-date prices.

Independent Swiss Snowsport Instructors (ISSI)

Inside the Viktoria Center, opposite the train station, +41 (0)27 967 70 67, 8am-10pm, www.issi.ch.

Number of instructors: seven
Private tuition: 160chf for two hours, 360chf for a full day (one-two people)
Max group size: eight
Ski guiding: 360chf for five hours (up to four people)
Children: children's lessons available

ISSI is a small school of snowboard and ski instructors. They only employ fully qualified instructors with years of experience. They have lessons suitable for all age groups and from beginner to advanced.

Prato Borni Ski & Snowboard School

Office located to the left of the Hotel Bahnhof, turn left out of the train station and walk 50m, +41 (0)27 967 51 15, www.pratoborni.ch.

Number of instructors: five
Private tuition: 195chf for two-and-a-half hours (one-two people) and 20chf per additional skier, 370chf for a full day and 30chf per additional skier
Children: they will pick your children up at your accommodation and offer lessons in all disciplines

New last winter, this small independent Swiss ski school offers well-qualified local instruction from a young friendly team. They offer private lessons in ski, snowboard and telemark for adults and children at all levels and also have a few mountain guides on their team should you want to explore the off-piste of the area.

Stoked

The office is opposite Migros supermarket on Hofmattstrasse, +41 (0)27 967 70 20, www.stoked.ch.

Number of instructors: around 90
Private tuition: 198chf for two-and-a-half hours and 20chf per additional skier
Max group size: eight for skiing, six for snowboarding
Group tuition: 165chf per person for three half days or 255chf for five half days. Reduced price for beginners
Children: Snowflakes Kids' Club (page 147),

Stoked was set up in 1994 as a snowboard school and has continued to grow ever since. They started teaching skiing in the winter of 2000/1. Last winter they had 90 instructors making them the second largest school in Zermatt. Predominately Swiss, there are a handful of British instructors in the team and the school offers a full range of adult groups and an extensive range of children's groups.

Summit Ski and Snowboard School

Office downstairs inside Perren Reinhold on the main street, +41 (0)27 967 0001, (photo opposite) www.summitskischool.com.

Number of instructors: 23
Private tuition: 240chf for three hours
Max group size: six
Group tuition: 125chf per person for a day, 290chf per person for four morning sessions
Children: 550chf per child for six full days (page 148).

Zermatt's first and only British ski school which means all lessons are taught in English. Summit is also unique in having a maximum of six people in any group lesson. Set up by three Brits who have worked in Zermatt for over 20 seasons between them, Summit provides for the English-speaking visitor with private and group lessons run for adults and kids at all levels. They also have popular one day coaching sessions that concentrate on one particular area of your technique helping you to move off your plateau.

Swiss Ski & Snowboard school

The office is located in the Alpine Centre on the main street, 8.30am-12pm, 3-7pm, +41 (0)27 966 24 66, www.skischulezermatt.ch.

Number of instructors: up to 260.
Private tuition: 160chf for two hours, 340chf for full day
Max group size: eight or nine (although sometimes more at peak times)
Group tuition: 310chf per adult for five days, 295chf for youths (13-20 year olds) for five days
Children: see page 148.

The original school has been going since 1929, with over 200 instructors and group lessons at all levels. While there is no guarantee how fluent your instructor's English will be, the size of the school makes them very flexible in terms of options and availability.

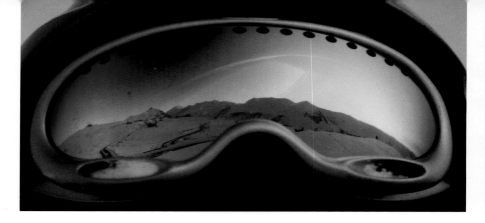

Equipment hire

All the ski shops in town will rent out similar standards of equipment at very similar prices. Bearing this in mind, it usually makes sense to choose a shop close to your hotel or chalet to make the beginning and end of the week that much easier. That said, there are some deals to be had; quite often your accommodation or ski school will have discounts available with certain shops. For example, if you have a lesson with Summit Ski School you can get 10% off equipment hire in Reinhold Perren Sports in the main street.

You can rent snowboarding equipment from most rental shops although Bayard Sport and Julen Sport have specialised shops. If you are after telemark gear then try either Anorak on the main street or Dorsaz Sport at the base of the Klein Matterhorn lift station.

Ski kit

Good kit is essential to keep you safe on the slopes. If you have any worries, or your rental boots feel unduly uncomfortable, you shouldn't worry about taking them back to the shop to change them.

Ski boots

Ski boots are awkward but they shouldn't be actually painful. When you are fitted, wear the socks you are going to ski in and keep your thermals and ski trousers out of the boot. Your feet will feel snug but make sure your toes don't touch the front of the boot when you are in the right skiing position - you should be able to wiggle them easily. Short toenails are essential,

otherwise they bang against the front of the boot (which hurts and can make the nail go black!). If you have any worries, or your rental boots are causing you pain, go and change them.

Snowboard boots

Snowboard boots are easier to walk in, softer than ski boots and straightforward to fit. They should be tight but not blood-stopping, your toes should just touch the end and your heels shouldn't lift too much. The harder, stiffer versions are best for off-piste.

Skis

Most skis are 'carving' skis and have a 'waist' so that if you put

them on their side and track them in the snow they draw a curve. This helps you turn more easily (rotate or tilt your feet to create an edge) making it quicker to learn and improve.

These skis are generally shorter than non-carving skis though off-piste skis are longer and wider (to help you 'float' in the powder). Slalom race skis can be as short as 160cm.

The binding of your skis has a number scale – the DIN setting – which dicatates how easily the binding releases your boots helping to avoid knee injuries; children, beginners and lighter adults will have a lower number.

Snowboards

Snowboards come in all shapes and sizes to cater for anything from the park (more flexible boards) to riding off-piste (stiffer boards) to ski touring ('splitboards'). If you are a beginner, the rental shop will generally give you a standard shaped board with a normal set-up on your bindings until you know what sort of riding you prefer.

Clothing

The best way to keep warm is by wearing layers. It's also sensible to carry a hat and an extra fleece in your rucksack in case the weather closes in. Needless to say, good glasses or goggles are essential (even on cloudy days) as the sun's rays are reflected by the snow and can damage unprotected eyes.

Good gloves or mittens are very important too. Early snowboarders particularly have to consider how waterproof their gloves and trousers are as they can spend a lot of time sitting down with their hands and bum in the snow! If you feel the cold, you can also buy glove liners.

Buy or rent?

The standard of rental equipment has improved loads so renting is a great option, especially if you want to try the latest skis. If you ski for more than a week or two a year, it's worth investing in custom-fit boots.

If you're thinking of buying your own kit, then check out end of season sales for good discounts of up to 50%.

This information was provided by Summit Ski and Snowboard School, Zermatt; www.summitskischool.com + 41 (0)27 967 0001.

Bayard Sport and Fashion

Main rental shop next to the station also specialises in snowboard rental. Four other shops set along the main street, 8am-12pm, 3-7pm, +41 (0)27 966 4960, www.bayardzermatt.ch.

A popular choice for equipment rental, Bayard also stocks a large selection of clothing by Mammut, Quiksilver and Prada, although the choices are on the expensive side.

Dorsaz Sport

Matterhorn base terminal, 8am-6.30pm, from 8.30am on Sundays, +41 (0)27 966 3810, www.dorsaz-sport.ch.

Rent ski, snowboard, telemark and touring gear from here as well as climbing, snowshoeing and Nordic walking equipment. Huge shop with loads of clothing and equipment to buy as well as a large rental selection. You can also leave your equipment with them after skiing to save carrying it back to your accommodation.

Julen Sport

Hofmattstrasse, next to the Vernissage, 8am-12pm, 2-7pm, +41 (0)27 967 4340, www.julensport.ch.

Wide selection of rental kit and clothing from Eider, O'Neill and more. You'll find an online reservation form on their website. Recommended for their boot fitting.

Matterhorn Sport

Bahnhofstrasse 78, main shop (clothing and rental) on the main street, two others at Steinmattstrasse 12 and Matterstrasse 59 (rental), 8am-12pm, 2-7pm, +41 (0)27 967 2956, www.matterhornsport.ch.

Great rental kit as well as one of the best selections in resort of hardware and clothing to buy such as Spyder, Napapijri and Westbeach. Online rental reservations available.

Perren Reinhold

Bahnhofstrasse, 8am-12pm, 2-7pm, +41 (0)27 967 2274, perren.reinhold@rhone.ch.

A sport shop with a large rental department and a good selection of rental ski and snowboard kit such as Volkl and Dynastar. Also home to Summit Ski and Snowboard School.

Slalom Sport

Two shops on Kirchstrasse 17, 8am-12pm, 2-7pm, +41 (0)27 966 2366, www.slalom-sport.ch.

Great for rental with a wide selection of equipment, friendly staff and excellent service. They have another shop on the same street selling their top-end rental and some of their more expensive clothing brands.

Piste ranking

The official piste ranking system, whilst useful, doesn't have enough detail for skiers looking for a challenge or early intermediates looking to avoid the more difficult slopes. And unfortunately, there's nothing but experience to tell you where to head to or avoid. Until now…

Mad Dog have teamed up with Summit Ski and Snowboard school to rank the **red**, **black** and downhill routes (shown on the piste map in yellow) in the Zermatt ski area using a star rating system:

   * = easier
  ** = average
*** = challenging

So you can now plan your day and head for the runs you want to ski. Useful for grading your progress, having competitions with your friends or just making sure you don't accidentally end up on a near-vertical icy black – our system is designed for skiers from early intermediate to advanced.

Reading the rankings

- Pistes are in numerical order and work from left to right on the piste map. Only pistes in the Zermatt ski area are reviewed here so you won't find information on those in Breuil-Cervinia
- Red pistes are shown first, followed by the harder black pistes, followed lastly by the unpisted downhill runs (shown in yellow on the piste map)
- The third column shows either lift or run which gives to access to each piste
- The connecting piste names have their number in brackets. The connecting lift has a letter which refers to the piste map

Summit ski and snowboard school

Since 2004, Summit Ski & Snowboard School has been offering high-quality private and group lessons to English-speaking visitors to Zermatt. They have a predominantly British team of very friendly, enthusiastic and qualified instructors. Summit's guarantee - that all group lessons are taught in English with a maximum of six in a group - has created a loyal following of clients. The success of the resort's first British ski school has seen their team grow to 20 instructors in the last two years. *+41 (0)27 967 0001, www.summitskischool.com.*

Apart from the gradient and width of the slopes, we have also taken a number of other factors into account:

- North or south? North-facing slopes are more inclined to be icy but keep snow longer
- Traffic – less busy pistes can

keep their snow longer but may not be pisted as often

- Grooming – the easier runs tend to be pisted more – some pistes are never groomed at all!
- Weather – how much snow it needs to work well as a piste and whether it is exposed to high winds

Red pistes

Piste	Comments	Connections
1 Untere National ★ ★	The best run down to town from the Sunnegga side – wide and rolling through the trees.	Patrullarve (D)
2 Ried ★	Nice and easy start then steepens and can often have big bumps for a short pitch before you reach the road.	Patrullarve (D)
4 Brunnjesch-bord ★ ★ ★	A fabulous red; long and wide. You can avoid the steepest section, halfway down, by following the path off on the right.	Sunnegga Express (A1)
9 Tuftern ★ ★	A fantastic long run when there is plenty of snow. Ends with a scenic path through the trees.	Patrullarve (D)
11 Rotweng ★ ★ ★	A classic red, with the opportunity to do some moguls on the side of the piste.	Rothorn (A3)
15 Tuftern-kumme ★ ★	Lovely in good snow conditions otherwise it can be a bit rocky. Follow it down to the Patrullarve chair for over 1000m vertical.	Kumme (14)
19 Fluhalp ★ ★	A long winding red which varies the whole way down. You can avoid the steepest pitch by following the road round to the right.	Rotweng (11)
26 Grünsee ★ ★	One short steep pitch at the start then onto a road which takes you past the Grünsee restaurant all the way round to Gant.	White Hare (28) Kelle (29)

Red pistes

Piste	Comments	Connections
27 Balmbrunnen ★★	Nice easy red that turns into a road; keep some speed up to avoid walking at the end.	**White Hare (28)** **Kelle (29)**
28 White Hare ★★★	Narrow winding piste at the top, can be intimidating for those uncomfortable with heights, then opens into a fantastic long and winding run.	Hohtälli (G)
29 Kelle ★★★	A great red that starts gently and then builds to a wide steep pitch down through a gulley.	Gifthittli Chair (M)
35 Gifthittli ★★	Watch out on this run to keep speed up over the flat sections at the start. Then enjoy the rolling steeper pitches down to the chair.	Gifthittli Chair (M)
39 Riffelalp ★★	Follow the piste through the tunnel and down alongside the railway. As the piste widens and steepens keep your speed up to help you across the flat.	Riffelberg (N1 and N2)
40 Riffelboden ★★	Classic red – handy if you are going to the Riffelalp train station, but not if you are planning on skiing down to Furi (or you will have quite a walk).	**Riffelalp (39)**
41 Landtunnel ★★	A nice winding run through the trees.	Riffelalp (N1)
42 Schweig-matten ★★	Solid red through the trees. As you near the bottom take the left fork to ski to Furi or the right one to ski to town.	Landtunnel (N1)

Red pistes

Piste	Comments	Connections
50 Blatten ★★	The run back to town from the Matterhorn side. Can get very crowded at the end of the day. Keep your speed up at the end to cut down the walking distance to the bus stop.	Furi (O1 or P1)
51 Weisse Perle ★★★	An alternative to the black run down to Furi. The steepest bits are very wide. Keep your speed up on the road to avoid walking.	Schwarzsee (P2)
52 Stafelalp ★	The first half is a stunning meandering run under the north face of the Matterhorn (great photo ops). After you pass restaurant Stafelalp (page 121), you will be on a winding road through the trees, where there are some sections you will need to walk.	**Weisse Perle (51)**
53 Oberer Tiefbach ★★★	A fantastic run that is almost always empty (because of the steep T-bar to access it).	Hornli T-bar (R)
55 Hirli ★★★	One steep narrow section in the middle always has big moguls on it, after that keep your speed up on the flat to avoid walking. Access is via a steep T-bar.	Hornli T-bar (R)
61 Skiweg ★	Not much of a run in itself, just a route from Schwarzsee to Furgg. Keep speed up near the end to avoid walking.	Schwarzsee (P2)

Red pistes

Piste	Comments	Connections
63 Sandiger Boden ★ ★ ★	Rolling steep red run, with great views down to town.	**Rennstrecke (65)** **Theodulsee (66)**
64 Garten ★ ★ ★	Fantastic wide and steep red, with big moguls off both sides of the piste.	**Rennstrecke (65)** **Theodulsee (66)** **Schusspiste (70)**
65 Rennstrecke ★ ★ ★	There is often a giant slalom (a race course with gates) course set up with timing - test your speed!	**Theodulsee (66)** Mid-station of Theodulgletscher chair (U1)
66 Theodulsee ★ ★	Gentle run, keep your speed up when the piste bends round to the right to get over the flat.	Trockener Steg (O2)
69 Matterhorn ★ ★	Easy meandering piste towards the east face of the Matterhorn. One narrow, steep section as you pass by the Matterhorn, after this keep your speed up to get to Furgg.	**Theodulgletscher (71)**
70 Schusspiste ★ ★ ★	Gentle at the top, great for carving, keep your speed up as it narrows to get across the flat, then the piste widens and steepens again.	**Theodulgletscher (71)**

Red pistes

Piste	Comments	Connections
71 Theodulg-letscher ★★	Fantastic long and open carving piste.	Furggsattel Chair (V)
72 Furggsattel ★★★	Same as **Theodulgletscher (71)** but on the other side of the chairlift. Access to snowpark on the right-hand side after the first steep section.	Furggsattel Chair (V)
74 Gandegghütte ★	A piste to access the Gandegghutte restaurant for lunch (page 113). Great views. Keep your speed up on the path to avoid a walk.	Gandegg (73)
80 Testa Grigia ★★	A wide run from Testa Grigia. Stay left if you want to head to Italy or right if you want to stay in Switzerland.	Testa Grigia (X2)
81 Führerpiste ★	Classic red that leads on to **Gandegg (73)**.	Plateau Rosa (83), Ventina Glacier (84)
82 Mittelpiste	Summer skiing only.	X6 or X7 T-bars
83 Plateau Rosa ★★	Wide rolling red run.	X4 or X5 T-bars
84 Ventina Glacier ★★	Same as **Plateau Rosa (83)** but on the other side of the T-bar.	X4 or X5 T-bars

Red/Black pistes

Piste	Comments	Connections
85 Matterhorn Glacierparadise ★★	Spectacular views from the top of Klein Matterhorn. An easy red that brings you close to the crevasses.	Klein Matterhorn Cable Car (03)

Piste	Comments	Connecting lifts
8 Obere National ★★	One of the best runs in the whole ski area. Long and rolling with some really steep pitches.	Blauherd (A2)
13 Downhill ★★★	Short but steep and off camber.	Rothhorn Cable Car (A3)
62 Furgg-Furi ★★	Fantastic, particularly early in the day (can get very busy in the afternoon as it's the only run down from this side to Furi).	Furgg (S)

Downhill routes

The yellow lines on the piste map ('downhill routes') are recognised pistes but are not groomed or patrolled. They are often steep and bumpy so are more suitable for the experienced skier. These pistes generally need a lot of snow to open and are also the first runs to be shut in dangerous conditions. It is also worth checking with your insurance company whether you are insured for these type of runs.

Piste	Comments	Connections
10 Paradise ★	A lovely rolling run that needs quite a lot of snow to be open.	Blauherd (A2)
16 Chamois ★★	An open run down the Rothorn face. Huge open run that feels like big mountain skiing. Best appreciated in powder or spring snow!	Rothorn (A3)
17 Marmotte ★★	Very similar to Chamois (16) but round to the side.	Rothorn (A3)
18 Arbzug ★★★	Quite an extreme little mogul run through the trees.	Tufternkumme (15)
20 Rio ★★	Great varied run through the trees back to town. Needs a lot of snow to be open.	Brunnjeschbord (4)
25 Berter ★★★	Bumpy and rugged run through the trees down to the Findeln chair.	Grünsee (26)

Piste	Comments	Connections
30 Mittelritz ★★	Fantastic, long and open bump run.	**White Hare (28)**
31 Platte ★★★	Similar to runs Triftji (33) and Stockhorn (34) but with narrower mogul gullies. Follow the path to have a break from the bumps.	Grieschumme (32)
32 Grieschumme ★★★	Similar to runs Triftji (33) and Stockhorn (34) but with narrower mogul gullies. Follow the path to have a break from the bumps.	Triftji (33) **Stockhorn (34)**
33 Triftji ★★★	Awesome bump run (or powder field if you get an early lift after a snowfall). Take the path after the first steep pitch if your thighs are burning.	Rote Nase Cable Car (H)
34 Stockhorn ★★★	This run has a short tricky start, and then opens up into a huge steep mogul field. Fantastic.	Stockhorn (L)
49 Bielti ★★	Winding, bumpy and narrow in parts… quite a lot of fun if you like that sort of thing.	**Weisse Perle (51)**
58 Hermetji ★★★	Steep bump run through the trees.	Aroleid mid station of Matterhorn Express (P2)

Piste	Comments	Connections
59 Tiefbach ★★★	Steep narrow bump runs down a gully, through the trees.	**Weisse Perle (51)**
67 Garten Buckelpiste ★★★	As steep as **Schusspiste (70)**, the red next door, but not pisted. Fantastic place to practice moguls or choppy snow.	**Schusspiste (70)**
68 Tumigu ★★★	Very similar to Garten Buckelpiste (see above).	**Schusspiste (70)**

Mad Dog day trips

Our day trips start around 9.30am and finish around 4pm. Timings are based on the pace of a competent red run skier and assume average length lift queues. Allow additional time if you are skiing more slowly or during school holidays when some lifts can have longer waiting times. If you are heading to Italy it is definitely better to be back over the border in good time rather than getting stuck with an expensive cab journey.

It is worth checking out the weather (page 38) at the start of your day to confirm that all the lifts are open and that you can ski the entire route as planned. If you are heading over to Italy, this area usually closes first in bad weather. If the weather closes in while you are out on the slopes, you can use the piste markers as guidance to find your way (see page 29).

Left/right directions on the piste assume you are heading down the hill. Directions for when you exit lifts refer to the way you are facing as you get off the lift.

Our researchers have worked hard to make these day trips as accurate as possible. However, pistes and routes can change from season to season so please make sure you take a copy of the piste map with you in case anything is unclear.

Day Trip 1 - Sunnegga, Gornergrat & Klein Matterhorn
This is a great way to start your week. The route will familiarise you with the ski area and really help you get your bearings.

Lift types

Lifts are shown with the symbols for the lift type:

Schlepplift	*T-bar*	
Sesselbahn	*Chairlift*	
Gondelbahn	*Gondola or bubble*	
Seilumlaufbahn	*Cable car*	
Standseilbahn	*Funicular*	
Bahn	*Train*	

Piste numbers and names are shown in the relevant colour; blue, red and **black**. The unpisted downhill routes are shown in yellow.

Day Trip 1 - Sunnegga, Gornergrat & Klein Matterhorn

Lifts	Comments
Sunnega Express (A1)	There are many different exits to this lift. Walk out of the tunnel at the bottom of the train, put on your skis and head right down the path to join the main piste **Brunnjeschbord (4)** down to the Patrullarve chairlift.
Patrullarve (D)	Turn right at the top and ski down to the cable car station at Blauherd.
Rothorn (A3)	Head straight down the piste, bearing right onto **Rotweng (11)** and then taking the left-hand turn follow the signs to Fluhalp. Ski down past the Fluhalp restaurant (good for lunch another day, page 111) to Gant.
Hohtälli (G)	Turn left at the top and head down the **White Hare (28)**. The top is a little narrow but soon opens out into a long beautiful run (the less confident can take the cable car straight across to Gornergrat). This is a long run so stop and take in the view from time to time. At the junction, turn left toward Riffelalp, and carry on until the Riffelalp Station.
Gornergrat Train (N2)	Get out at the first stop, Riffelberg, and ski around the back of the restaurant to the Gifthittli chairlift.

Lifts	Comments
Gifthittli (M)	Turn right at the top and ski down **Gornergrat (36)** back towards Riffelberg. Here, head through the tunnel under the train past the bottom of the Gifthittli chair and follow the path to the right through another tunnel. The piste brings you around past the 5-star Riffelalp Resort Hotel. Head down past the tree line to Furi. At the end of the piste head over the bridge, take your skis off and walk uphill for about a minute to Restaurant Simi.
Lunch	**Restaurant Simi (page 120, +41 (0)27 967 2695).** Walk another few hundred metres and turn left into the tunnel below the Furi station. Take the elevator up and walk around to the cable car.
Furi-Trockener Steg (02)	Turn left and walk to the Klein Matterhorn cable car.
Trockener Steg-Klein Matterhorn (03)	Walk down the tunnel (slowly it is nearly 4000m high!). From the top the views across to Switzerland, Italy and France are amazing and you can see all the way to Mont Blanc. Take the run down, staying right, and it will lead you all the way back to Trockener Steg.

Lifts	Comments
Furggsattel (V)	Take the left-hand piste at the top and turn left about halfway down. Follow this all the way to Furgg (for a less steep variation ski around via Trockener Steg). Whichever route you choose, you will end up at Furgg, where you'll find the gondola to Schwarzsee in the lift station.
Furgg-Schwarzsee (S)	Turn left out of the top and take the **Weisse Perle (51)** all the way back to Furi. Keep a little speed on the last section, as it is quite flat. From Furi take the piste **Blatten (50)** towards town but be careful as it can be very busy at the end of the day. Almost at the bottom you'll find your après-ski stop.
Après-ski	**Hënnu Stall, a wild après-ski bar with a live band in the spring – perfect for drinking glühwein (page 96).** Continue on the piste back to town.

Day trip 2 - Klein Matterhorn & Breuil-Cervinia

A chance to ski in two countries in one day. Start the morning by heading up to the Klein Matterhorn and ski over to Italy for some fantastic runs in the sun, followed by a delicious Italian lunch. Perfect for a beautiful day.

Note: bring your passport as you are crossing country borders. Also bring euros if you have them, although most restaurants and hot-chocolate stops take Swiss francs. Before you leave Zermatt, check that you have an international pass; if not you can get a daily upgrade (37chf from the bottom of the Matterhorn Express).

Day trip 2 - Klein Matterhorn & Breuil-Cervinia

Lifts	Comments
Matterhorn Express (P1) 📷	Try and start your day just before 9am or after 10am to avoid the ski school rush and the crowds trying to get over to Italy. Take the Matterhorn Express gondola and make sure you get out at Furi; don't carry on up to Schwarzsee.
Furi-Trockener Steg(02) 📷	At Furi, change onto the Furi-Trockener Steg cable car. Think thin; this cable car takes 120 and it can be a bit of a squash.
Klein Matterhorn (03) 📷	At Trockener Steg head to your last cable car of the morning that takes you up to the Klein Matterhorn. If the queue is too long or you don't like heights, take T-bars X1 and X2 up to Plateau Rosa instead, but you do miss out on some stunning views.
	Once up at Klein, it is worth taking a few minutes to absorb the breathtaking views; almost 4000m and the highest piste in Europe. Before you descend, see if you can spot Mont Blanc (past the Matterhorn on the left, the huge white one) and some of the other famous peaks.
	Once skiing, follow the piste down **Matterhorn Glacier Paradise (85)** which then turns into **Ventina Glacier (84)**. As you ski down next to the T-bar (X4 and X5) look over to your left and take this you'll see a piste heading along a relative flat path to Plateau Rosa/Testa Grigia (a cable car station and group of buildings on the border with Italy).

Lifts	Comments
	At Plateau Rosa turn left and enter Italy (if you go right, and ski down next to the T-bar, you can either head back to Trockener Steg or take a later left-hand turn for an easier piste into Italy).
	Follow the **Ventina (7)** all the way down to Breuil-Cervinia. The Ventina is one of the best runs in the whole ski area so savour the steep pitches and wide sections as you ski the 14km long run. You'll pass various junctions on the way down but, unless you want to do an extra loop on a chairlift, just keep following signs to Breuil-Cervinia.
Breuil-Cervinia–Plan Maison (A)	Once in Breuil-Cervinia you will arrive at a lift station with both a gondola and a cable car (they both go to the same place but the gondola is much quicker). Take the gondola (A) up to Plan Maison (this is the central hub of the Italian side).
Plan Maison (N)	Take the 4-man covered chairlift which you will see as you look up the mountain. Lunch is a short ski down from the top of this chairlift, so if it is still early, you can take the next chair (or two) up to get a bit more mileage.
	Follow the main piste down (blue – 6), keeping left. About half way down (towards Plan Maison) you will see a chalet tucked into the mountain side; this is your lunch spot.
Lunch	Chalet Etoile – (page 108, +39 166 940220). An alternative option for lunch is **Bontadini** (see page 107) at the top of the second chair.

Lifts	Comments
	Make sure you leave lunch in time to catch the last lifts back to Zermatt. The times of the last lift change throughout the winter: 3pm up to the end of January and then 3.30pm.
Plan Maison (N) 🚡	At Plan Maison take the 4-man covered chair.
Fornet (O) 🚡	When you get off the chair you will see another to get on that will take you further up towards the Swiss border.
Bontandini (P) 🚡	After the second chair, you will see the last 4-man covered chair up. At the top, get off to the right-hand side. Ski about 15m and take the turning to the left (back onto the Swiss side) under the building.
	Follow the path round and you will join up with a main red run **Testa Grigia (80)** that turns into a long flat blue run, **Gandegg (73)**. It is worth getting a bit of speed up here so you don't need to walk along the flat.
	As you ski down the blue run you will see Trockener Steg ahead of you. Follow the piste all the way there and then onto **Theodulsee (66)**. There is a split in the piste about halfway down, but it doesn't matter which path you choose as both will take you to Furgg.

Lifts	Comments
	At Furgg, follow the piste around the back of the cable car building and take the black run **Furgg-Furi (62)** down from there. This is a fantastic run (although admittedly best done in the morning as it can get quite busy at the end of the day). If you would like to ski more, you can take the chairlift up and get another ski down to Furgg.
	If you would rather not ski the black, enter the cable car station at Furgg and take the gondola up to Schwarzsee, and take the **Weisse Perle (51)** down to Furi.
	Once at Furi, follow the final piste, **Blatten (red – 50)**, down towards Zermatt. Follow the piste back to the Matterhorn Express lift station in town where you will find a bus stop and taxi rank.
Après-ski	**Papperla Pub, a lively après-ski bar with regular live bands and a handy ski/board check area (page 97).**

Day trip 3 - The Matterhorn Ski Safari

This route has been put together by the tourist office and gives you the chance to ski the entire international ski area in one day without having to use the same lift or run twice. On completion of this route you will have skied 10,000 vertical metres. You can pick up Matterhorn Ski Safari piste maps at most lift stations.

Note: bring your passport as you are crossing country borders. Also bring euros if you have them, although most restaurants and hot-chocolate stops take Swiss francs. Before you leave Zermatt, check that you have an international pass; if not you can get a daily upgrade (37chf from the bottom of the Matterhorn Express).

Day trip 3 - The Matterhorn Ski Safari

Lifts	Comments
Sunnega Express (A1) 🚡	There are many different exits to this lift: get out on the left (as you are looking up the train) and take the left-hand exit to the escalator. Here you will take the Sunnegga-Blauherd 'chondola' (a lift that alternates gondolas and chairs).
Sunnegga-Blauherd (A2) 🚠 🚡	At Blauherd, put your skis on and ski down **Standard (7)** back to Sunnegga. Then continue round the Sunnegga lift station and restaurant to join the main piste **Brunnjeschbord (4)**, down to the Patrullarve chair.
	If you prefer a harder ski, from Blauherd follow **Standard (7)** but watch out for the **National (8)** on your right-hand side, and take this all the way to the Patrullarve chair.
Patrullarve (D) 🚡	Turn right at the top and ski down to the cable car station at Blauherd.
Rothorn (A3) 🚠	Head straight down the piste, bearing right onto **Rotweng (11)** and then taking the left-hand turn follow the signs to **Fluhalp (19)**. Ski down past the Fluhalp restaurant (page 111) to Gant.
Hohtälli (G) 🚠	Turn left at the top and head down the **White Hare (28)**. The top is a little narrow but soon opens out into a beautiful run (the less confident can take the cable car straight across to Gornergrat). This is a long run so you may want to stop and take in the view from time to time. At the junction, turn left toward Riffelalp, and carry on until the Riffelalp Station.

Lifts	Comments
Gornergrat Train (N2)	Get out at the first stop, Riffelberg, and ski around the back of the restaurant to the Gifthittli chairlift.
Gifthittli (M)	Turn right at the top and ski down **Gornergrat (36)** back toward Riffelberg, head through the tunnel under the train past the bottom of the Gifthittli chair and follow the path to the right through another tunnel. The piste **Riffelalp (39)** brings you around past the 5-star Riffelalp Resort Hotel. Head down past the tree line to Furi. At the end of the piste take the fork to the left and head over the bridge. Take your skis off and walk uphill for about a minute to Restaurant Simi.
Break	**Restaurant Simi (page 120).**
	Walk on another few hundred metres and turn left into the tunnel below the Furi station. Take the elevator up and walk around to the gondola.
Furi – Schwarzsee (P2)	At the top of the gondola follow **Skiweg (61)**, on the left, round to Furgg.

Lifts	Comments
Theodulgletscher (U1/2)	When you get off the chair ski down and take the left-hand turn, follow the piste across the T-bar round to Trockener Steg. Once you cross the T-bar keep some speed as it's very flat.
Trockener Steg-Klein Matterhorn (03)	Walk down the tunnel (slowly as it's nearly 4000m high). From the top here the views across to Switzerland, Italy and France are amazing; you can see all the way to Mont Blanc.
	Once skiing, follow **Matterhorn Glacier Paradise (85)** down to the T-bars (X4 and X5). Follow the piste down past the bottom of the T-bars, **Plateau Rosa (83)** then **Führerpiste (81)**, and watch out for the turning on the left to another T-bar (Testa 1 - X2) that heads up to Plateau Rosa.
Testa 1 (X2)	At Plateau Rosa look ahead and you will see Testa Grigia, your lunch stop.
Lunch	Testa Grigia – (page 121, +39 166 94 83 69). **Visit the smarter restaurant downstairs or just grab a delicious panini or snack upstairs.**
	After lunch, follow the **Ventina (7)** down to the right all the way to Breuil-Cervinia. You'll pass various junctions on the way down but, unless you want to do an extra loop on a chair, just keep following signs to Breuil-Cervinia.

Lifts	Comments
Breuil-Cervinia–Plan Maison (A) 🚡	Once in Breuil-Cervinia you will arrive at a lift station with both a gondola and a cable car (they both go to the same place but the gondola is much quicker). Take the gondola (A) up to Plan Maison. Without leaving the station follow the signs to the bubble for Laghi Cime Bianche.
Plan Maison-Laghi Cime Bianche (T) 🚡	When you arrive, stay in the station and head to the cable car up to Testa Grigia.
Laghi Cime Bianche–Testa Grigia (F) 🚡	Take the **Testa Grigia (80)** down on the left as you exit the station and ski down next to the T-bar. After the piste crosses the T-bar watch out for the left-hand turning back into Italy.
	Follow the pistes down (there are lots of different options but just keep aiming for Plan Maison at the bottom of the three chairlifts).
Plan Maison (N) 🚡	At Plan Maison get on the 4-man covered chair.
Fornet (0) 🚡	When you get off the chair you will see another to get on that will take you further up towards the Swiss border.

Lifts	Comments
Bontandini (P)	After the second chair, you will see the last 4-man covered chair up. At the top get off the chair to the right-hand side. Ski about 15m and take the turning to the left (back onto the Swiss side) under the building.
	Follow the path round and you will join up with **Testa Grigia (80)** that turns into a long flat run **Gandegg (73)**. It is worth getting a bit of speed up here so you don't need to walk along the flat.
	As you ski down the blue run you will see Trockener Steg ahead of you. Follow the piste all the way there. Once there take the 6-man chair.
Furggsattel (V)	As you ski down the piste splits, take the left-hand fork onto **Theodulgletscher (71)**. About halfway down take the left-hand piste **Schusspiste (70)**, and follow this all the way to Furgg.
Furgg-Schwarzsee (S)	Turn left out of the top and take the **Weisse Perle (51)** all the way back to Furi. Keep a little speed up on the last section as it is very flat.
	From Furi take the piste **Blatten (50)** towards town. Be careful as it can be very busy at the end of the day. Follow the piste back to the bus stop in town.
Après-ski	**Elsie's Bar (page 96) for some upmarket après-ski involving champagne and oysters (page xx).**

After all your hard work on the slopes, you deserve some decent **food and drink.** Here's our inside view on the best places to refuel.

What you'll find in this chapter...

Take the traditional Alpine fare of cheeses, cured meats and potatoes and add to it the loving attention of a guild of professional chefs and the result is a ski haven of culinary excellence.

In many resorts, it is difficult to find food that isn't stodgy, heavy and cheese-based. However, Zermatt excels here, providing a whole range of tastes from Thai to African to Japanese… there's even a McDonalds for you to avoid.

Restaurant prices tend to reflect Zermatt's reputation of being a pricey resort, although the standard of cuisine is generally high so you do get your money's worth. There are a few cheaper eateries in the pizza/pasta/fondue category which also serve good-value food (page 80). If you are on a budget, also check out the supermarkets' surprisingly good range of fresh food (page 137). On the other end of the scale, if you want to splash the cash and have a special meal, there are restaurants in Zermatt that will blow your expectations, as well as your wallet.

Vegetarian options

Although there are vegetarian dishes on most restaurant menus, there are only so many times that someone can eat pasta with tomato sauce or pesto in a week. Because of this, we've highlighted restaurants **V** that diversify their vegetarian options a little bit. And of course, there is always the staple of cheese to fall back on - cheese fondues and raclettes are widely available. If you eat fish, there are often plenty of fish dishes available too.

Children

Most restaurants offer either children's menus or half-priced, half-portion versions of their main dishes. We've included a selection of particularly family-friendly choices in the **Children** chapter (page 141).

75

On the other end of the scale, if you want to splash the cash and have a special meal, there are restaurants in Zermatt that will blow your expectations, as well as your wallet.

Swiss food:

Cheese fondue:	a mixture of cheeses and alcohol in a bubbling cauldron that keeps the mixture molten whilst you dip bread into it. It can normally only be ordered for a minimum of two.
Käseschnitte:	a melted cheese sandwich that is covered in white wine and cheese and baked in the oven. Sometimes served with ham or eggs.
Knoblauchsuppe in Brot:	A garlic soup served in Valais bread. Served at the highest hotel in the Alps – the Kulm Gornergrat (page 20) to help with altitude sickness.
Meat fondue:	a bubbling cauldron of oil which you dip cubes of meat into and cook to your preference. It can normally only be ordered for a minimum of two.
Raclette:	a chunk of raclette cheese is set up on your table next to a burner. As the heat melts the top layer of cheese, scrap it onto your plate of meats and potatoes. Take care not to let it burn! It can normally only be ordered for a minimum of two.
Rösti:	a national dish in Switzerland, rösti is grated potato made into patties and then fried or baked. Served with a variety of options such as eggs, ham or vegetables. Great comfort food!
Zermatter heusuppe:	Valais speciality of soup made with hay that has a (nice) hay-like taste and is a green/brown colour. Served in traditional Zermatt restaurants.

Swiss drinks:

Glühwein:	the famous après-ski drink of hot mulled red wine – perfect for those chilly days where you need warmth, sugar and alcohol, all in one glass.
Kirsch:	a Swiss schnapps made from cherries.
Schumli pflumli:	a sort of Alpine Irish coffe. Zermatt bars and restaurants specialise in many different types of coffee, usually with alcohol.
Williamine:	pear schnapps designed to go with your beer whilst you're still in ski boots; generally helps you to forget about dinner time.

Swiss wine

When the subject of Swiss wine comes up, most tourists tend to know little or nothing of the subject. A country better known for cheese and chocolate, Switzerland also has a long history of vine cultivation and wine making. Archaeologists in the region have found grape seeds while excavating ancient communities that existed as long ago as 10,000 B.C.

This small nation is made up of 26 different cantons (states) – six of which produce wine; Valais, Vaud, Geneva, Neuchatel, Ticino and Zurich. The Valais, home to Zermatt and Verbier, is the largest wine producing region in Switzerland and you'll find a wide variety of wines available in the resorts. The guide prices given below are for shops; expect to pay two to three times more in restaurants.

The wine most popular and representative of the varied soils and climates in the Valais is Fendant (15-25chf), made from the chasselas grape. Simple in style but perfect with fondue and raclette, or as an aperitif, Fendant varies from village to village in the Valais; Sierre for 'exquisite' bitterness, Sion for freshness and richness, Ardon and Vetroz for stimulating dryness, Leytron and Saillon for fruity smell and Martigny for bouquet. Petite Arvine (20-35chf), a local variety, is extremely elegant in style, slightly salty on the palate, off dry with notes of honey and minerality - perfect with seafood or a strong cheese. If possible indulge in one of the delicious sweet/dessert wines made from Petite Arvine, (H)Ermitage (Marsanne Blanche) or Malvoisie (Pinot Gris). They are simply wonderful with foie gras and dried figs.

Red wines are definitely the surprise package of the local wines. From the racy fruitiness and structure of Pinot Noir from Salquenen, to the spicy complexity of the Syrah (Shiraz) from the village of Chamoson, there is a Swiss wine for every occasion. Dole (15-25chf), a blend of Pinot Noir and Gamay, is the most common red of the Valais. From Martigny to Salquenen this wine varies considerably in style and structure. Producers in Martigny rely on the lively and fruity qualities of Gamay, whilst those in Salquenen emphasize the structure and power of Pinot Noir. Dried meats and Dole are a match made in heaven. Of particular interest perhaps is the oldest local variety in the Valais, Cornalin (25-40chf). Deep in colour, Cornalin has a gorgeous bouquet, and packs a punch that is a match for any modern red

wine. Try it with a hearty meat dish or simply on its own.

But please, don't stop at these options, try the many other wines of the regions from the wild and savage Humagne Rouge to the silky texture of the Johannisberg (white). The Valais is truly a wine lover's voyage of discovery!

This introduction to Swiss wines was provided by **Peter Beaty**.
Wine Maker - Cave Fin Bec
Wine Consultant/Importer & Retailer
peterbeaty@hotmail.com
+41 (0)79 680 5953 (Verbier)
Zermatt
Welschen Getränke, Spissstrasse 26 & Hofmattstrasse 14
Page 138

Budget meals and take-aways

Food in general is fairly expensive in Zermatt but there are always budget choices, especially if you're happy with pizza and pasta. A lot of bars such as Potter's Bar (page 98) and the North Wall (page 97) also have food that, although basic, work well on a budget. And it's always worth checking out menu deals or promotional offers in mid-priced restaurants as these are usually great value.

Take-aways tend to be a cheap option but, again, choices are limited. Outlets such as the Crêperie (page 85) and the Brown Cow (page 83) offer snacks and more substantial dishes that can be taken away. Supermarkets, especially Coop (page 137), offer a wide range of fresh produce including sandwiches and salads.

On the mountain, self-service restaurants are cheaper choices and provide a quicker meal allowing you to get back on the slopes. Alternatively, buy your lunch from the town bakeries, delicatessens and supermarkets (pages 137-139) and eat alfresco on the slopes.

Resort restaurants

The main street in Zermatt has restaurants every few yards as varied as the Old Spaghetti Factory (page 87) and the 5-star Mont Cervin Grill (page 87). However, if you prefer to get off the beaten track a little, there are also some great finds on almost every street or alleyway, try the China Garden (page 84) or Le Mazot (page 86). Wander down past the side of the church and you will find another bustling street of restaurants including one of our favourites, The Pipe (page 88).

The better the restaurant, the earlier you will need to reserve – sometimes even as early as you book your holiday. The loyal followers of these places return en masse year in, year out. Wednesdays and Thursdays are chalet staff night off - and tables get booked up fast - so it's definitely worth pre-booking these nights (or asking your host to) at the start of your holiday.

Reading our reviews:

Resort restaurants (page 83) and bars (page 95) are listed in alphabetical order. Unlike with mountain restaurants (page 105) we only include reviews of resort restaurants we recommend.

 – budget: majority of main course prices are under 8-20chf

 – mid-range: majority of main course prices range from 21-35chf

 – expensive: majority of main course prices are 35chf and above

 – good vegetarian choices

 – venues that close late (1am or after)

 – our absolute **Mad Dog favourites**. These are the places that our researchers return to time and time again; sometimes for their classic mountain feel, sometimes for their warm welcome, sometimes for their budget prices and sometimes because they're perfect for a treat.

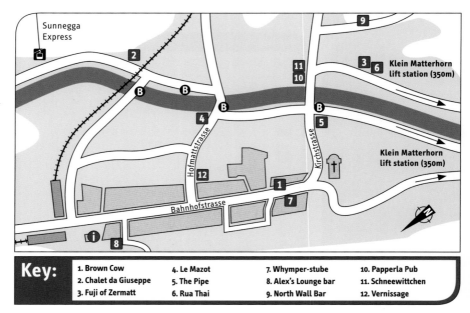

Key:

1. Brown Cow
2. Chalet da Giuseppe
3. Fuji of Zermatt
4. Le Mazot
5. The Pipe
6. Rua Thai
7. Whymper-stube
8. Alex's Lounge bar
9. North Wall Bar
10. Papperla Pub
11. Schneewittchen
12. Vernissage

Our absolute favourites...	and why
Brown Cow – page 83.	Budget but good quality snack food in a comfortable setting
Chalet da Giuseppe – page 84.	Special occasion restaurant that serves an exciting menu
Fuji of Zermatt – page 85.	Expensive but a great place for sushi and teppanyaki
Le Mazot – page 86.	Smart and cosy traditional restaurant specialising in lamb dishes
The Pipe – page 88.	Innovative African, Asian and Indian fusion menu providing the perfect break from the usual Alpine fare
Rua Thai – page 90.	Huge menu and excellent surroundings
Whymper-stube – page 91.	Eat luscious fondues at one of the locals' favourites

Brown Cow – Postli Snack Bar
T: +41 (0)27 967 1931
W: www.hotelpost.ch

Hotel Post, Bahnhofstrasse 41, on the main street near the Alpine Centre, 9am–2am.

Fuel up on budget food with choices such as club sandwiches (12.50chf), potato skins (9.50chf) or lasagne (19.50chf). Pizzas can also be ordered from the Pizzeria Broken next door (page 88). The Brown Cow is a great place to meet up for a relaxing après-ski or, if the weather is bad, spend a warm comfortable day here. Take-aways also available.

Casa Rustica

T: +41 (0)27 967 4858
W: www.casarustica.ch

Bahnhofplatz 46, 50m turn left out of the station square away from town – walk 50m and the restaurant is on the right, 11am-10pm.

Traditional rustic Swiss venue serving meaty dishes: veal steak with morels and noodles (44chf), duck in orange sauce with rice (34chf) and salad with lamb fillet, rocket and parmesan (17.50chf). The food is excellent but unlikely to suit vegetarians, although their carrot or wine soups are well worth a try.

Chalet da Giuseppe

T: +41 (0)27 967 1380

Vispastrasse 28, along the river opposite Admiral Hotel, 6pm-1.30am.

An often-recommended Italian set next to the rushing river, Giuseppe's offers a warm ambience, some tasty inventive a la carte cuisine and attentive service. Try the four-course 'surprise menu' at 68chf or order off the extensive menu with dishes such as a starter of ravioli of asparagus, scampi and Aragosta salsa (28chf) or the fillet of St. Pietro (John Dory) with champagne and shrimps (35chf). Definitely one for a special night out.

China Garden

T: +41 (0)27 966 4610
W: www.chinagarden-zermatt.ch

Bahnhofstrasse 18, just off the main street behind Raiffeisenbank, 12–2pm, 6pm–midnight.

This Chinese restaurant has a pleasant ambience and friendly service. The chicken with Szechwan pepper sauce (27chf), crispy fried duck with garlic sauce (32chf) are good choices. Vegetarian dishes include tofu and mushroom soup (15chf) or omelette with pickled cabbage (15chf). Good value group menus offered. Wine prices start at 42chf for a bottle of Fendant or Dole at 45chf.

Crêperie

T: +41 (0)27 967 1091

Bahnhofstrasse, walk up the main street away from the train station. the crêperie is on your right almost opposite the Mont Cervin Palace, 1-10pm.

Tempting customers as they walk by the window, the crêpes here are excellent and the variety of fillings huge. Try savoury ham and cheese or sweet choices such as chocolate and banana. The Crêperie also serves up some delicious milkshakes as well as ice cream when the sun is shining. Perfect for a little bit of indulgence or as a quick budget snack.

Fuji of Zermatt

T: +41 (0)27 966 6171
W: www.hotelalbanareal.com

Hotel Albana Real, Schluhmattstrasse 19, by the river on the way to Klein Matterhorn lift terminal, 11.30am-2pm, 6-11pm.

Extremely popular but expensive Japanese teppanyaki restaurant with a sushi bar. Fantastic food - Californian maki sushi (10chf for 8) or Teppanyaki red snapper (21chf). There are a variety of sushi menus of offer. Children can have half-portions of the main menu. The food combined with oriental décor and atmosphere makes this a popular eating place. Book in advance.

Il Ristorante

T: +41 (0)27 966 4611
W: www.walliserkanne.ch

Bahnhofstrasse 23, 6.30pm–midnight.

Expensive but excellent Italian food with mouth-watering dishes. Try the fillet of beef with black truffle juice (45chf) or perhaps saffron risotto with asparagus and parma ham (25chf). They also have daily specials such as venison fillet with foxberry sauce (42chf) and veal escalope with lemon and pistachio butter (39chf). Vegetarians have a range of risotto or pasta, for example ravioli with mushroom and herbs (25chf). Wine prices start at 45chf.

Le Mazot
T: +41 (0)27 966 0606
W: www.lemazotzermatt.ch

Hofmattstrasse 23, 6-11pm.

This grill restaurant is fairly expensive but worth it for a treat. Famous for their lamb (try saddle of lamb with rosemary crust, 38chf) this carnivore-orientated restaurant won't disappoint. Vegetarians aren't forgotten however, with salads (17chf), noodles (18chf), and the usual pasta dishes. The restaurant achieves a smart but cosy and traditional ambience with knowledgeable waiters and excellent service. Advance booking essential.

Mont Cervin Grill

T: +41 (0)27 967 8888

W: www.seiler-hotels.ch

Mont Cervin Palace, Bahnhofstrasse, 12-2.30pm, 7-11pm.

An exclusive restaurant whose loyal following tend to book up months in advance, especially during peak season. With an elegant Alpine restaurant setting, the starters comprise delicacies such as baby langoustine on carpaccio of pink grapefruit (25chf), or tasty vegetarian options of ravioli of fresh cheese with lemon and thyme sauce (26chf). Main courses from the charcoal grill include leg of suckling pig or half saddle of veal.

North Wall Bar

T: +41 (0)27 966 3412

W: www.northwallbar.com

Hotel Rhodania, Staldenweg, walk down Kirchstrasse and turn right on the second street after the bridge, 6.30pm-12.30am.

Serves pizzas (from 12chf) and nachos (9chf) – perfect for a cheap eat with your beer. See also nightlife review on page 97.

Old Spaghetti Factory

T: +41 (0)27 967 1931

W: www.hotelpost.ch

Hotel Post, Bahnhofstrasse 41, on the main street near the Alpine Centre, 6–11pm.

A fun and lively restaurant with a huge menu such as tagliatelle with giant shrimps (25.50chf), fillet of lamb with Italian herb sauce (32chf) or veal escalope with lemon and butter (32chf). Vegetarians have choices of pasta such as spaghetti with broccoli, tomatoes and garlic and tagliatelle with rocket and lemon. Pizzas are also available on request though they're not shown on the menu.

The Pipe

T: +41 (0)79 758 5324
W: www.chakralounge.com

Kirchstrasse 38, 4.30pm–midnight, 6–10.30pm for full dinner menu.

An excellent fusion restaurant with influences from India, Asia and Africa. Try Cape Malay curry (33chf), wasabi jumbo shrimp salad (22/31chf) and Sri Lanken vegetable korma (27chf). Caters for large bookings (10% discount for 10 people or more). Open for après-ski as well as serving snacks and drinks after dinner service. They also organise sledge fondue nights from Furi.

Pizzeria Broken

T: +41 (0)27 967 1931
W: www.hotelpost.ch

Hotel Post, Bahnhofstrasse 41, on the main street near the Alpine Centre, 6pm–1.30am.

A wide selection of pizza or choose from pasta dishes including lasagne or tortellini with spinach and ricotta. Great place to bring the kids as they can make their own pizzas – mini pizzas available from 11.50chf, large ones from 13.50chf. Traditional wood-fired ovens make their pizzas delicious. Part of the Hotel Post complex, this is an lively and entertaining restaurant.

Restaurant du Pont
T: +41 (0)27 967 4343
W: www.dupont-zermatt.com

Oberdorfstrasse 7, just past the church (heading away from the train station), at crossroads, 11am-10pm.

A simple wooden shack-like restaurant with atmosphere and charm, helped along by lots of candles and friendly staff. Rather an unusual mixture of music; Swiss accordion/choral/country, but somehow not too intrusive. The food is simple and homemade; rösti, ham and egg (17chf) and a variety of fondues.

Rua Thai
T: +41 (0)27 966 6181
W: www.hotelalbanareal.com

*Hotel Albana Real,
Schluhmattstrasse 19, 11.30am-
2pm, 6-10pm.*

A huge menu - containing delights
such as fried ravioli or chicken with
hot basil and chilli (27chf) - means
deciding what to have can be
difficult. However, help is at hand
from the set menus available. The
atmosphere is fantastic and is a
welcome change from the usual
traditional restaurants. The only
downside is that the service can
occasionally be a little hit and miss.

Restaurant Stockhorn
T: +41 (0)27 967 1747
T: www.grill-stockhorn.ch
(German only)

*Hotel Stockhorn, Riedstrasse 22,
follow Kirchstrasse until it turns into
Riedstrasse, 6.30-10pm.*

A good value grill restaurant with
budget to mid-price meals and a
lively ambiance. The Stockhorn
cooks the meat over an open wood
fire for a wonderful flavour. Meat
and cheese fondues as well as
raclettes are available. The
restaurant is set over two floors and
a word of warning – if you don't
love the smell of cheese fondue,
eat upstairs.

Swiss Chalet
T: +41 (0)27 967 5855

*Bahnhofstrasse, just behind
Raiffeisenbank, look out for sign on
the main street, 6pm – midnight.*

Traditional Swiss restaurant set just
off the main thoroughfare of
Zermatt, the Swiss Chalet serves an
interesting take on the usual fare of
fondue: curry, pineapple and
cheese fondue (23chf pp). Other
main dishes include pork steak
with herb butter (26chf), or lamb
steak with gratin (34chf). Fish
dishes include trout in white wine
(32chf). Vegetarians have the
option of fondues, röstis or salads.
Wine starts at 38chf a bottle.

Walliserkanne

T: +41 (0)27 966 4610
W: www.walliserkanne.ch

Bahnhofstrasse 32, 6–10pm.

A mid-priced place for families and big groups, this is a loud and busy restaurant with a varied menu from pizzas (22chf) to pasta (20chf) to steak (34chf). Vegetarians are well catered for with offerings such as cannelloni with ricotta and spinach (22chf).

Whymper-stube

T: +41 (0)27 967 2296
W: www.whymper-stube.ch

Under the Monte Rosa hotel on Bahnhofstrasse, 3pm–1am.

When in the Alps, do as the Alpine folk do, and eat fondue. The meaty fondue Bourguignonne (40chf pp) and the luscious sounding (and tasting) gorgonzola fondue (24chf pp) are just a selection of those on offer; you can't go wrong here. Popular amongst locals and tourists alike, you will need to get in quick with your reservation.

Après-ski and nightlife

Après-ski is traditionally a big part of the skiing holiday with many people stopping on the way home from an exhausting day on the slopes to refuel and recharge before tackling dinner.

The famous Hënnu Stall (page 96) on the slope back into town from Furi - is a popular lively venue while the neighbouring Zum See (page 123) is great for those that prefer something a little more sedate.

Down in resort, there are a choice of bars that kick off for both après-ski as well as après-dinner such as the champagne and oyster orientated Elsie's Bar (page 97) or the more affordable Papperla Pub (page 97) where you can carry on well into the night.

As night falls, central Zermatt steps up the pace and people spill out of the bars onto the streets. As well as these choices, it is definitely worth dropping into the trendy Vernissage (page 99) or perhaps going for a cocktail in the slightly surreal lounge bar of the Hotel Alex with a different style corner to suit every mood (page 95).

Bars and clubs are usually free to enter unless there is a particular party on or it's New Year's eve.

> **How read our reviews:**
>
> – budget: large beer costs around 5chf
>
> – mid-range: large beer costs between 6-7chf
>
> – expensive: large beer costs over 8chf
>
> – venues that close late (1am or after)
>
> – our absolute **Mad Dog** favourites (page 81)

Live music

These bars have bands playing regularly although it is worth checking times and dates with them as details can change throughout the season:

Alex's Lounge Bar – page 95.	A band performs in the relaxed lounge bar on Tuesday nights playing all the classics
Hënnu Stall – page 96.	Live bands play at the après-ski hut on warmer afternoons
Olympia Stübli – page 116.	Live bands most afternoons in the spring
Papperla Pub – page 97.	Live bands play regularly at this young hang-out
The Pink Live Music Bar – page 98.	Jazz, blues, soul and funk bands play every night of the week
Schneewittchen – page 98.	Live bands play on Sunday nights in this nightclub
The T-Bar – page 99.	Regular live bands playing Irish music and rock and roll
Vernissage – page 99.	Live rock and pop bands play on occasion; check with the venue for dates

Our favourite bars and clubs

Alex's Lounge Bar – page 95.

Welcoming bar with a wide range of quality drinks, attracting a slightly older crowd

North Wall Bar – page 97.

Budget option in a young, friendly and skiing-orientated crowd

Papperla Pub – page 97.

Lively bar for après-ski or for later in the evening

Schneewittchen – page 98.

Dance until the early hours in this popular nightclub

Vernissage – page 99.

An über-cool bar - sip cocktails and nibble tapas with friends

Alex's Lounge Bar

T: +41 (0)27 966 7070
W: www.hotelalexzermatt.com

Bodmenstrasse 12, Turn right out of the station onto the main street and take the first right, 10am-2am.

The Hotel Alex's bar is a favourite with UK tourists and a great place for those who like an extensive drinks list and comfortable surroundings. The bar has wines from all over the world and a large number of whiskeys and cocktails (although drinks are expensive with a large beer coming in at 9chf). The atmosphere is warm and homely with corners decorated in different themes, such as the tartan clad Scottish corner. There is also internet, live music (page 93) and a pool table to keep you busy.

Broken Bar Disco

T: +41 (0)27 967 1931
W: www.hotelpost.ch

Hotel Post, Bahnhofstrasse 41, on the main street near the Alpine Centre, 10pm-3.30am.

Part of the huge Hotel Post complex on the main street, the Broken Bar is located under the oldest vaulted cellar roof in the village. One of the most famous clubs in town, you can dance away on a wine barrel to a variety of hit cheesy songs and anthems.

Brown Cow Snack Bar

T: +41 (0)27 967 1931
W: www.hotelpost.ch

Hotel Post, Bahnhofstrasse 41, on the main street near the Alpine Centre, 9am-2am.

A comfortable and popular bar for the day or night and a great place for meeting friends. House wine starts at 3.50chf a glass. It also serves a good range of budget meals such as club sandwiches, snacks and even pizza from the Pizzeria Broken next door. Take-aways also available (page 83).

Country Bar

T: +41 (0)27 967 1596

W: www.elite-zermatt.ch

 【LATE】

Hotel Elite, follow Hofmattstrasse down past the ice rink, the bar is on the right after the second crossroads, 6pm-2am.

The Country Bar is tucked away underneath the Hotel Elite and is where you will find those in need of a game of pool. They also have internet access if you want to catch up on your email (page 130).

Elsie's

T: +41 (0)27 967 2431

W: www.elsiebar.ch

 【LATE】

Bahnhofstrasse, opposite the church, 4pm-2am.

Set in a small old building bursting with character, you can enjoy après-ski in style in the upmarket Elsie's Bar. Champagne and oysters are their speciality but other choices include caviar and cocktails (long drinks cost from 15chf). You can book a table through their website.

Hënnu Stall

T: +41 (0)27 966 3510

W: www.hennustall.ch

On the piste from Furi to town, 2-7pm.

This is one of the busiest après-ski places in Zermatt; the bar is always packed and the drinks flowing. A wild après-ski bar with plenty of atmosphere, the chalet-style building is lovely and warm inside and perfect for drinking hot chocolate or glühwein on a freezing day. The terrace is great fun on warm spring afternoons when you can listen to the live band, order a ski of shots (10 shots from 50chf) and try to dance in your ski boots.

North Wall Bar
T: +41 (0)27 966 3412
W: www.northwallbar.com

Hotel Rhodania, Staldenweg, walk down Kirchstrasse and turn right on the second street after the bridge, 6.30pm-12.30am.

The North Wall bar attracts a mixed crowd of extreme skiers, season workers and holidaymakers, who come here for the reasonable prices and buzzing atmosphere. The décor is very simple but the atmosphere is friendly and there are regular drink specials, pizzas and nachos. The atmosphere is lively and you can be sure they'll be showing skiing or climbing videos.

Papa Caesar's Lounge Bar
T: +41 (0)27 967 1931
W: www.hotelpost.ch

Hotel Post, Bahnhofstrasse 41, on the main street near the Alpine Centre, 6pm-2am.

A cosy first floor lounge bar that's pleasant to relax in with a cocktail or two. The prices are expensive but the ambience makes it worth paying the extra few francs.

Papperla Pub
T: +41 (0)27 967 4040
W: www.papperlapub.ch

Steinmattenstrasse 34, walk over the bridge away from town on

*Kirchstrasse and you'll see the pub
on your left, 2.30pm-2am.*

Fantastic mid-priced après-ski
bar/pub with an outdoor area
complete with new hot tub that
gets pretty lively during warmer
afternoons. There is also a handy
ski/board check area to keep your
equipment safe while you drink.
Inside, the crowd dances away to
live bands. Party nights, DJs and
jamming sessions are regular here.
A menu of snacks, salads and
main dishes are available for the
peckish. Try the ribs cooked in
Jack Daniels (21chf). If you want to
carry on until the early hours, then
head downstairs to the
Schneewittchen nightclub.

The Pink Live Music Bar
T: +41 (0)27 967 1931
W: www.hotelpost.ch

*Hotel Post, Bahnhofstrasse 41, on
the main street near the Alpine
Centre, 8pm-2am.*

Enjoy live music ranging from pop
to gospel and rock to jazz in an
upmarket sophisticated venue.

Potter's Bar
T: +41 (0)27 967 6595

*Viktoria Center, opposite the train
station, 9am-12pm.*

New for last season, Potter's Bar bills

itself as Zermatt's only English bar. It
serves Guinness and Strongbow
(both 6chf) and has an old-
fashioned wooden pub feel to it. As
well as the English breakfasts, live
sport and bingo nights, Potter's
injects a bit of an international feel
by serving homemade grappa (5chf)
and putting on fondue nights. Good
for groups and parties looking for an
intimate but friendly night.

Schneewittchen
T: +41 (0)27 967 4040
W: www.papperlapub.ch

*Steinmattenstrasse 34, walk over
the bridge away from town on
Kirchstrasse and you'll see the*

nightclub on your left, next to Papperla Pub, 8pm-3.30am.

In the basement of the Papperla Pub, this is the best nightclub in town with great music to suit all tastes and a fantastic dance floor. Head down here after warming up in the popular Papperla Pub – just upstairs. Famous for their themed parties and live bands on Sunday nights, this is the place to come to really let your hair down and shake your stuff. The more extroverted can even practise their pole dancing but everyone has the chance to make new friends in here. Try and keep quiet at chucking out time as it's right in the middle of a group of hotels.

The T-Bar
T: +41 (0)27 966 4000
W: www.reconline.ch/pollux.

Bahnhofstrasse, underneath the Hotel Pollux, 9am-3.30am.

A lively bar with an inviting atmosphere. They often have live music with bands playing a mix of Irish tunes and rock and roll.

Vernissage
T: +41 (0)27 967 6636
W: www.vernissage-zermatt.ch.

Hofmattstrasse 4, opposite floodlit ice rink, 5pm-2am (4am for parties).

A stunning lounge bar ideal for the early evening with leather sofas, ambient music and tapas (12-35chf) to indulge in. Turns into one of the busiest clubs, often with international DJs on their infamous party nights. For more information, see page 13 and page 127.

Village Dance Club
T: +41 (0)27 967 1931
W: www.hotelpost.ch

Hotel Post, Bahnhofstrasse 41, on the main street near the Alpine Centre, 11pm-3.30am.

Dance to the latest hits in this Hotel Post nightclub.

Mountain restaurants

Zermatt's mountain restaurants use imagination and flair when it comes to their ingredients. Cuisine on the mountain tends to be split into Swiss and Italian traditional Alpine food with pasta and polenta dishes featuring heavily.

Because you don't always know where you'll end up on the mountain, we review all the restaurants that are accessible by piste in the Zermatt ski area, whether good, bad or indifferent. Mountain restaurants are listed by sector (Sunnegga, Gornergrat, Klein Matterhorn) and from left to right on the piste map (page 102). We've also included a few places in Breuil-Cervinia that we think you'll particularly like.

Generally, the closer to the border you ski, the more Italian the cuisine. You will see from our reviews that Zermatt's mountain restaurants use imagination and flair when it comes to their ingredients. Prices are more uniform but on balance more expensive than in resort although, in most restaurants, you will get your money's worth.

It is advisable to take cash with you or to check when booking that the restaurant accepts credit cards. The restaurants on the Italian side of the ski area accept Swiss francs as well as euros. Advanced booking is necessary at most of the restaurants especially at peak holiday times although the larger restaurants and those that offer self-service accept walk-ins.

Most restaurants open and close with the lifts, although food service is likely to finish after lunchtime (a little later in self-service places). If opening or food service times differ substantially to this, we say so.

Finding your restaurant:

We review all the restaurants marked on your piste map within the Zermatt ski area. We've also included those over on the Breuil-Cervinia side that we recommend in our day trips (starting page 63).

Rather unhelpfully, restaurants appear on the map as a knife and fork symbol, rather than by name so we have created our own map (page 102) with each restaurant numbered in **red**. These numbers are shown next to each of our reviews.

Zermatt also has some great places to eat that are not shown on the piste map but are very close to the piste. We have included these too and numbered them in **blue**.

Where restaurants are also accessible for pedestrians, we tell you. However, there are a few of them that you can only reach on skis/board or if you are hiking/snowshoeing.

Restaurants

1	Ried	23	Riffelberg Hotel
2	Othmar's Hütte	24	Gornergrat Restaurant
3	Tufternalp	25	Jägerstube Zmutt
4	Restaurant Rothorn	26	Schwarzsee Hotel
5	Restaurant Blauherd	27	Furgg Käsestube
6	Restaurant Sunnegga	28	Pizzeria Cervino /
7	Fluhalp		Trockener Steg
8	Adler	29	Gandegghütte
9	Paradies	30	Stafelalp
10	Chez Vrony	31	Theodul Hütte
11	Enzian	32	Testa Grigia
12	Findlerhof	33	Bontadini
13	Grünsee	34	Chalet Etoile
14	Restaurant Alm		
15	Hënnu Stall	1	Olympia Stübli
16	Riffelalp Resort	2	Moos
17	Alphitta	3	Farmerhaus
18	Chämi-Hitta	4	Gitz-Gadi (Hotel Silvana)
19	Restaurant Ritti	5	Marmottes
20	Restaurant Simi	6	Aroleid
21	Blatten	7	Restaurant Furri
22	Zum See		

Our favourite mountain restaurants

Alphitta, Gornergrat – page 106.	A rustic restaurant serving classic favourites
Blatten, Matterhorn – page 106.	Expensive but good-value fare with imaginative vegetarian dishes
Chalet Etoile, Breuil-Cervinia – page 108.	Fabulously friendly and relaxed restaurant on the Italian side
Chez Vrony, Sunnegga – page 109.	Scenic restaurant with a special atmosphere where a particular effort is made for children
Findlerhof, Sunnegga – page 110.	Has a solid reputation for creative food and a warm welcome
Fluhalp, Sunnegga – page 111.	All-round favourite for its atmosphere and food – and perfect for a sunny day
Marmottes, Matterhorn – page 115.	New arrival that has earned a following in its first year
Testa Grigia, Matterhorn – page 121.	Italian restaurant perched on the border – polenta and rustic cheese salad dishes make this a winner
Zum See, Matterhorn – page 123.	A must-visit for any foodie

Adler (8)

T: +41 (0)27 967 1058

*Lifts: from Sunnegga, ski **Easy Run** (6) into the hamlet of Findeln. When piste reaches a path, turn right and restaurant is ahead of you, Pedestrian: from Sunnegga, there is a walking trail down to Findeln, follow path for about 15 minutes to Adler.*

There are some amazing views from this restaurant and, although it can be expensive, there are some well-priced options too. Dishes include aubergine and courgette salad with rocket and truffles (23chf) as well as homemade spaghetti with king prawns and mussels (27chf) and venison with mustard (38chf).

Restaurant Alexandre (Riffelalp Resort) (16)

T: +41 (0)27 966 0555

*Lifts: ski **Riffelalp (39)** from Riffelberg and stop at the 5-star Riffelalp Resort, Pedestrian: Gornergrat train to Riffelalp, then follow path towards hotel (about 10 minutes), Food service: 12pm-2.30pm, 7.15-9.30pm.*

One of the more upmarket restaurants in the Riffelalp Resort and definitely worth dining here for the views. Dishes on offer include fillet of sea bream Mediterranean style (36chf) or try the escalope of veal with ham and masala gravy (36chf). A three-course menu here costs around 80chf.

Restaurant Alm (14)

T: +41 (0)27 967 1646

*Lifts: from Gornergrat, ski towards Furi on **Schweigmatten** (42); just before you reach the road, take fork off to the right and restaurant is about 20m along, Pedestrian: Matterhorn Express to Furi and follow road back towards town (about 10 minutes), Food service: lunchtimes and Friday evening for sledging dinners.*

Famous for their fresh trout, this restaurant has many other fish dishes such as salmon lasagne (15chf) or fish soup with trout (8chf). The large menu means there is definitely something for everyone. House wine from 44chf.

Alphitta (17)
T: +41 (0)27 967 2114

*Lifts: from Riffelalp, ski **Landtunnel (41)** towards Furi and about 10m below Riffelalp, the restaurant is on your right, Pedestrian: Gornergrat train to Riffelalp and then walk 10 minutes down to just below.*

Delightfully rustic and busy, this is the best restaurant on the Gornergrat side. The service is welcoming and the food includes favourites such as steak and chips (32chf), lamb and rösti (30chf) and large salads (15chf). Vegetarian options include pasta with pesto (20chf), tomato soup (10chf) or rösti with fried eggs (15chf). **No credit cards**.

Aroleid (6)
T: +41 (0)27 967 2658

*Lifts: from Schwarzsee, ski **Weisse Perle (51)** or **Furgg-Furi (62)** from Furgg, Pedestrian: from the Furi lift station the easiest option is to walk up the side of the piste, it's about 100m up on your left, Food service: 10am to the evening.*

A family-run restaurant with a small menu containing simple but traditional Swiss mountain food such as a selection of rösti (12.80-15.30chf). Their käseschnitte (13.80–15.80chf) is reputed to be the best in the region. The restaurant's interior is small but there is a lovely terrace to soak up the sun. **No credit cards**.

Blatten (21)
T: +41 (0)27 967 2096

*Lifts: from Furi, ski halfway down **Blatten (50)**, restaurant is on the right-hand side, Pedestrian: on walking path between town and Furi (20 minutes up from town, 10 minutes down from Furi).*

Generally an expensive restaurant but with tasty dishes and roast chicken on Sundays. Lovely terrace with cushioned benches and rugs to snuggle up under. It also has clean (almost luxury) toilets in a separate outhouse. Good range of vegetarian options including mushroom soup covered with puff pastry. A quieter après-ski stop than nearby Hënnu Stall.

Bontadini (33)
T: +39 335 250312

Lifts: top of chairlift 'O' and bottom of chairlift 'P', Pedestrian: no access.

This restaurant on the Italian side has a lovely atmosphere and provides baskets of freshly baked bread and tasty canapés while you order. The regularly-changing menu includes delights such as carpaccio with rocket and grana cheese (€16), and mixed antipasto of the valley (€13). The food is delicious and the portions generous, the only downside is that the service can be a bit slow. The self-service section also serves great food. House wine from €15.

Restaurant Blauherd (5)
T: +41 (0)27 967 3524

Lifts/Pedestrian: top of Sunnegga–Blauherd chondola (A2).

This mid-priced self-service restaurant can be extremely busy, especially with various ski and snowboard school groups that lunch there. Not the most attractive of restaurants but it works well as a quick budget lunch stop serving staples such as spaghetti bolognaise (18chf), and pizzas (from 15chp) bratwurst and chips (17chf). Watch out – the floor can get incredibly slippery. Check out the terrace, where live bands play on sunny days, making it an ideal spot to soak up the atmosphere and the sun.

Chalet Etoile (34)
T: +39 166 940220

Lifts: Plan Maison (N) chair, follow the main blue piste down keeping left. About halfway down (towards Plan Maison) you will see a chalet tucked into the mountain side, Pedestrian: no access.

On the Italian side, this is an unmissable lunch stop although make sure you book. The terrace is roomy but the restaurant is so cosy and welcoming on snowy days that you'll want to stay the afternoon. The recent non-smoking laws make the restaurant a pleasant place to spend time in. The Swedish owner has been here for almost 30 years, and the food is unmistakably Italian with great fresh fish options (€15-20) especially on Wednesdays, including linguine with scampi for €15. One of the house specials is an impressive 'bird' made out of silver foil containing porcini mushrooms, shrimps, and black truffle sauce. Leave room for the delicious desserts at just €5 including unbeatable green apple sorbet with calvados. If you cannot manage a dessert, try the 'manga e bevi' grappa with red berries (amazing even if you don't like grappa). Cheese and meat plates, chicken or caprese salad all at just €9. If you don't have time to savour the restaurant experience they also have a smaller self-service area.

Chämi-Hitta (18)
T: +41 (0)27 967 1096

*Lifts: from Riffelalp, ski towards Furi on **Landtunnel (41)**, Pedestrian: from Riffelalp train stop walk towards the Riffelalp Resort. Take path on right.*

Lovely warm atmosphere with friendly staff and excellent traditional food such as käseschnitte and interesting vegetarian dishes – mixed salad with mushrooms in puff pastry (22chf). Their conservatory allows you to enjoy the views even on colder days. It's also an ideal après-ski stop from the Gornergrat side with a wide range of coffees and hot drinks. From 32chf for a litre of wine.

Chez Vrony (10)
T: +41 (0)27 967 2552

Lifts: from Sunnegga, ski Easy Run (6) down into Findeln, and to the restaurant, Pedestrian: from Sunnegga, there is a walking trail to Findeln (about 25 minutes to restaurant).

A warm atmosphere with very friendly staff and a wonderful ambience. The superb food includes five specials each week such as calf's liver or saffron risotto with shrimps and chorizo. A good place to take children (page xx). Relax in the sun loungers on the terrace with a wonderful view of the Matterhorn.

Enzian (11)
T: +41 (0)27 967 6404

*Lifts: from Sunnegga, ski Easy Run
(6) down into the hamlet of
Findeln, close to end of the run,
Enzian is on right-hand side,
Pedestrian: from Sunnegga, there
is a walking trail down to Findeln,
follow path for about 30 minutes.*

Fairly basic food in an informal
atmosphere: soup (10chf), rösti
with tomato, cheese and egg
(21chf) or pasta with pesto (20chf).
Dish of the day can include
homemade quiches (21chf),
calf's liver (27chf) or lamb fillet
37chf). House wine served from
35chf per litre.

Farmerhaus (3)
T: +41 (0)27 967 3996

*Lifts: from Furi, restaurant is at top
of Blatten (50), just under Furi lift
station, Pedestrian: Matterhorn
Express, walk down to the bottom
of right-hand path.*

Traditional local fare including
many different types of rösti as well
as käseschnitte dishes. Pizzas and
meat cooked on the grill are also
on offer. Half-portions are available
for children. The restaurant has a
great location and large restaurant
(both inside and out) with
traditional chalet décor inside. On
the whole the service is good but it
can be a little slow.

Findlerhof – Franz & Heidi (12)
T: +41 (0)27 967 2588

*Lifts: from Sunnegga Express, ski
Easy Run (6) – follow sign near end
of piste for Findlerhof, leave skis
against the barn (stadel) and follow
path, Pedestrian: from Sunnegga
follow walking trail down to Findeln
(30 minutes).*

A superb restaurant in every way,
Findlerhof is situated in the
beautiful hamlet of Findeln
amongst the stadels, with fantastic
views towards the Matterhorn. As
well as many rooms inside and
several layers of terracing outside,
there is also a conservatory for
colder weather. The food and

service are exemplary and Franz and Heidi themselves make sure your meal is nothing but perfect. The wine menu is reasonably priced and you'll want to return to this gem of a restaurant. Try the pot au feu (25chf), the beef carpaccio with asparagus and scampi (36chf) or the ravioli with herbs and truffle cream sauce (24chf). From 38chf for a litre of wine.

Fluhalp (7)
T: +41 (0)27 967 2597

*Lifts: from Rothorn, ski **Rotweng** (11), stay right at first fork then follow down, turning left onto trail - **Fluhalp (19)**. Stay on trail until you see Fluhalp, a big building with red shutters, Pedestrian: no easy access.*

Excellent friendly service and fantastic food: white asparagus with salmon (37chf), veal steak with cep sauce (37chf) and salad with avocado, mango and king prawns (27chf). The sunny terrace hosts a live band in the spring. Wine from 35chf.

Furgg Käsestube (27)
T: +41 (0)27 967 6195

 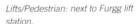

Lifts/Pedestrian: next to Furgg lift station.

The slogan of this restaurant is 'welcome to a world of cheese', so no surprises that it is best known for its fondues and raclettes. Not a place for fine dining but the food is good and reasonably priced so perfect for a quick lunch stop. The terrace is great in the spring when they sometimes have an outside grill going. Self-service also available.

Restaurant Furri (7)

T: +41 (0)27 966 2777

Lifts/Pedestrian: outside the Furi lift station.

Usual fare of salads (7-15chf), rösti (14-19chf) and pasta (14.50-19chf). They also serve a range of vegetarian dishes such as cannelloni with spinach (19chf) and vegetable omelette (16chf). A great place to stop for a coffee either mid-morning or mid-afternoon. For those with a sweet tooth, they have a wonderful selection of tempting homemade tarts for just 4.50chf. In Spring their huge terrace is perfect for sun bathing.

Gandegghütte (29)
T: +41 (0)79 607 8868

*Lifts: Gandegg T-bar (X1) up from Trockener Steg; get off at mid-station. When skiing down the run, take the right onto **Gandegghütte (74)** to the restaurant. Keep your speed up to avoid a walk. Pedestrian: no access.*

Good traditional food at a fair price; a nice alternative to the self-service at Trockener Steg. The mountain hut is rustic and simple but it has great views over the Theodul Glacier to the Breithorn. Dishes include Bavern omlette with bacon and tomato (19chf) and käseschnitte Gandegg (17.50chf).

Gitz-Gadi (Hotel Silvana) (4)
T: +41 (0)27 966 2800

*Lifts: from Schwarzsee, follow **Weisse Perle (51)** down to Furi, at the end of the path through the trees, restaurant is on left-hand side, Pedestrian: from Furi lift station, follow road up the hill for 10 minutes and restaurant is on your left, Food service: 11.30am-5pm, dinner available between 7-8pm.*

This restaurant has a special ambience with a fireplace and cosy atmosphere as well as a terrace for warmer days. The food is great with decent size portions. House wine starts from 39chf.

Gornergrat Restaurant (24)
T: +41 (0)27 966 6400

Lifts/Pedestrian: top of Gornergrat train, take elevator up into shopping centre, Kulm Gornergrat hotel and restaurant complex.

The Gornergrat complex has recently undergone a makeover resulting in a much better looking space. The restaurant has a formal but friendly atmosphere and good food including veal schnitzel (36chf), tortelloni with spinach and ricotta (21chf). The children's menu has options such as chicken nuggets (11chf) and hot dogs (10chf). There is also a modern and spacious self-service section.

Grünsee (13)
T: +41 (0)27 967 2553

Lifts: from Hohtälli, ski White Hare (28) or from Gornergrat, ski Kelle (29) in the direction of Gant. Grünsee is on right-hand side just above the tree line, Pedestrian: no access.

A run-of-the-mill mountain restaurant, the food is basic (Rösti, käseschnitte and pasta – you aren't going to find an inventive dish here) and the ambiance is fine. There is nothing particularly special nor dire about this place. The terrace is huge and in the spring they have deckchairs out if you need to work on your ski tan.

Hënnu Stall – Après-ski hut (15)
T: +41 (0)27 966 3510

On the piste from Furi to town, 2-7pm, www.hennustall.ch.

This is one of the busiest après-ski places in town; the bar is always packed and lively and the drinks flowing. See page 96.

**Restaurant Jägerstube Zmutt
(Hunter's Parlour) (25)**
T: +41 (0)27 967 1241

*Lifts/Pedestrian: pedestrian access
only, walking trail through Zmutt
hamlet, one hours' walk up from
Zermatt or 40 minutes' walk down
from Furi, Food service: 10am-
5.30pm.*

Enjoy the tranquillity of this hidden
restaurant accessible only on foot.
Soak up the views whilst sampling
the local cuisine. The basic fare on
offer includes fondues, rösti and
pasta but this helps to reinforce the
feeling of being in the middle of
nowhere.

Marmottes (5)
T: +41 (0)27 967 8282

*Lifts: from Furgg, ski **Furgg-Furi
(62)** to bottom to find restaurant or
ski **Weisse Perle (51)** from
Schwarzsee and near Furi, look out
for sign on right, Pedestrian:
Matterhorn Express to Furi, five
minutes' walk up the piste, Food
service: 11.30am-4pm, evening
meals available for 15 plus people.*

A new arrival last season that has
been extremely popular from the
start. The staff are young and
professional and the food
wonderful with specialities such as
venison, mussels with asparagus in
lobster sauce and rösti with

salmon. Vegetarians are catered for
with dishes including Asian
noodles with vegetable (21chf) and
half-portions are available for
children. The décor is chalet-like
without being dark and
claustrophobic; instead the
restaurant is light and inviting.
Generally quite expensive but with
some well-priced dishes available.
House wine starts at 48chf.

Moos (2)

T: +41 (0)27 967 4770

Lifts: Matterhorn Express to Furi, then ski down round the lift station over the bridge. Then walk up about 50m to piste Moos (43). Alternatively, you can ski down from the Gornergrat side and meet piste Moos (43), Pedestrian: walk down from Furi towards town and you will pass the restaurant, Food service: 11am-8pm.

Very friendly atmosphere and great food including peppered steak (32chf), salad with lamb (25chf) and penne arrabiata (17chf). And of course, lots of types of rösti. House wine starts at 35chf.

Olympia Stübli (1)

T: +41 (0)27 967 2407

Lifts: Sunnegga Express (A1), take Brunnjeschbord (4) past bottom of Patrullarve chair (D) and down Untere National (1), piste turns into path and Olympia is further down on the right-hand side, Pedestrian: 20 minutes' walk up from town, Food service: 11am to après-ski, evening meals available.

An English-friendly restaurant with amazing views over the town to the Matterhorn from the sun terrace. Dishes served include Tuscan onion soup, homemade spag bol and the usual salads and burgers. With a live band most afternoons in

the spring, there is a fantastic atmosphere perfect after a hard day on the slopes. Vegetarians and children are catered for well.

Othmar's Hütte (2)

T: +41 (0)27 967 1761

Lifts: from Sunnegga (A1), take Brunnjeschbord (4) to bottom of Patrullarve chair (D). Continue down to Zermatt, taking right-hand piste Ried (2) and restaurant is about 200m down on left-hand side, Pedestrian: no easy access, Food service: 10am-7pm (evening dining also possible).

With main courses ranging from 15chf to 43chf, this restaurant is a good choice for groups with differing budgets. Renowed for their fish dishes such as Alaskan salmon, halibut and king crab legs. House wine starts at 34chf per bottle.

Paradies (9)
T: +41 (0)27 967 3451

*Lifts: from Sunnegga, ski **Easy Run** (6) down into Findeln. After the path at the start of the piste, you'll see a signpost to Paradies on left, Pedestrian access: from Sunnegga, follow the walking trail down to Findeln (15 minutes), evening bookings are available for groups – make sure you phone in advance.*

Dishes of the day include calf's liver with rösti (34chf) and fillet of beef served on a hot stone (45chf). Imaginative vegetarian dishes: such as salad with caramelised pears and Roquefort (21.50chf) and homemade cheese spatzli (19.50chf). Children's portions are available for 10chf. Soak up the rays in the deckchairs on the terrace.

Pizzeria Cervino (28)

T: +41 (0)27 967 1812

Lifts/Pedestrian: in the Trockener Steg building.

A popular place for skiers on the Klein Matterhorn side that don't want to eat in the self-service or ski down to Furi for lunch. The pizzas are excellent (the Biagio has parma ham, rocket, fresh tomatoes and parmesan). Vegetarians have the option of different variations of pizza and pasta. Small portions are available for children. The restaurant can get extremely busy at times, leading to a long wait for food. Avoid the noise on busy days by eating out on the terrace overlooking the Matterhorn.

Ried (1)

T: +41 (0)27 967 4284

*Lifts: from Sunnegga (A1), take **Brunnjeschbord (4)** to bottom of Patrullarve chair (D). Continue down taking right-hand piste **Ried (2)**, once piste turns into a path look out for restaurant on right-hand side, Pedestrian: no easy access, Food service: 11am-7pm.*

Relaxed and friendly atmosphere serving food such as braised cabbage with potatoes and sausages (20chf) and meaty farmer fondues (25chf). Vegetarian choices include vegetable strudel (21chf). Children's options include sausage skewers or meatballs (11chf).

Riffelalp Pavillion Terrace (Riffelalp Resort) (16)

T: +41 (0)27 966 0555

*Lifts: ski **Riffelalp (39)** from Riffelberg and stop at the 5-star Riffelalp Resort, Pedestrian: Gornergrat train to Riffelalp, then follow path towards hotel (about 10 minutes).*

This restaurant is more geared towards skiers wanting a lunch stop on the mountain than the more upmarket hotel restaurant here. With the usual mid-priced pizzas, pastas and grill dishes, this is a middle-of-the-road choice. Sit on the terrace on sunny days and admire the views.

Riffelberg Hotel Restaurant (23)
T: +41 (0)27 966 6500

Lifts/Pedestrian: located in the large building with red shutters just below the Riffelberg stop.

A light open-plan restaurant with huge windows looking over to the Matterhorn and, although not particularly big, it has a terrace to seat more on sunnier days. Service is friendly and the food reliable and well presented. Dishes include sliced pork and noodles (25chf) and rösti with pears, vegetables, cheese and fried egg (19.50chf).

Riffelberg Self-Service Restaurant (23)
T: +41 (0)27 966 6500

Lifts/Pedestrian: located in the large building with red shutters just below the Riffelberg stop.

A large and busy restaurant that serves well as a quick and cheap lunch stop. Inside, it's full of kids in ski school and is generally loud and crowded making the large terrace a better option on sunnier days. Dishes include bratwurst (15chf), schnitzel (19chf) and spaghetti bolognaise (16chf). No booking necessary.

Restaurant Ritti (19)
T: +41 (0)27 967 1482

*Lifts: from Gornergrat, ski towards Furi on **Schweigmatten (42)**; just before you reach the road up to Furi, take right-hand side path to Ritti (path goes uphill for 200m), Pedestrian: no easy access.*

Not the easiest place to get to but the prices are cheaper than other mountain restaurants and the traditional food is good (especially the rösti with bacon for 15chf and cheese fondue, 44chf for two). Enjoy the beautiful views across to Furi. House wine from 44chf.

Restaurant Rothorn (4)
T: +41 (0)27 967 2675

Lifts/Pedestrian: top of the cable car to Rothorn (A3).

An enjoyable high altitude choice for lunch on the Sunnegga side with friendly service and reasonable food. Choices include for instance lasagne (19.50chf) , fillet steak with croquettes (32chf), and chicken salad (19.50chf). Although quite a trek up from town (1500m vertical) the views are fantastic and there's a conservatory to allow you to soak up the views on colder days. Very child-friendly – they serve half portions of the main menu. House wine starts at 39chf for one litre.

Schwarzsee Hotel Restaurant (26)
T: +41 (0)27 967 2263

Lifts/Pedestrian: in hotel at top of Schwarzsee.

This restaurant has fantastic views and good food such as smoked trout (24chf) as well as the usual mountain fare. There is also a self-service section with a similar menu to the restaurant but at a couple of francs cheaper.

Restaurant Simi (20)
T: +41 (0)27 967 2695

*Lifts: from Gornergrat, ski towards Furi on **Schweigmatten (42)**; when the run turns into **Moos (43)**, the restaurant is on your left, Pedestrian: between Furi and town.*

This conveniently located restaurant has a sun trap of a terrace, The extensive menu has expensive choices as well as some budget dishes (soups are 6.50chf or 12chf for goulash soup, pot au feu for 17chf and rösti in all its many varieities for 17-19chf). You can also choose more unusual main course such as sweet and sour prawns for 26chf. The wine list suits all budgets. If you're stopping here mid-afternoon you might want to make use of one of the very comfortable sun-loungers on the terrace.

Stafelalp (30)
T: +41 (0)27 967 3062

*Lifts: top of Schwarzsee, ski piste
Stafelalp (52) to the restaurant,
Pedestrian: no access, Food
service: 10am-6pm.*

The prices are mid-range and the
food very traditional (ie lots of
cheese options!) but the location is
spectacular. It's right under the
north face of the Matterhorn giving
you wonderful views. The restaurant
has a traditional mountain hut
ambiance (wooden throughout with
benches and stuffed animals on the
walls). The terrace is large and
perfect for spring afternoons.

Restaurant Sunnegga (6)
T: +41 (0)27 967 3046

*Lifts/Pedestrian: top of Sunnegga
Express (A1).*

Busy but spacious restaurant,
easily accessible making it a useful
place to meet up with beginners
and non-skiers. Often full of groups
of children so the restaurant can
be noisy and the service
sometimes slow. Not the place to
go for a gourmet mountain lunch
but reasonably priced and it has a
large range of food such as
spaghetti with smoked salmon
(22.50chf). Relax on the great sun
terrace in the spring.

Testa Grigia (32)
T: +39 166 948 369

*Lifts: Plateau Rosa, top of X2 T-bar
or top of cable car (F) from Breuil-
Cervinia, Pedestrian: no access.*

Delightful sunny restaurant with a
panoramic view of the surrounding
glacier, Testa Grigia makes a good
lunch or pit stop when heading over
to/back from Italy. The first floor
restaurant serves an Italian menu
featuring cured meats, cheeses and
polenta dishes. Also on offer is a
huge starter of warm cheeses (€14).
Vegetarian options are plentiful and
there is a daily changing set menu.
Wine starts from €12.

Theodul Hütte (31)

Lifts: top of chairlift (P) from Breuil-Cervinia, Pedestrian: no access.

This restaurant perches on the Italian-Swiss border and so has wonderful sweeping views across both ski areas. Unfortunately, it is only easy to access from the Italian side and so isn't an ideal lunch stop. The food is unremarkable and includes the usual fare of pasta, cheese and meats.

Trockener Steg (28)

T: +41 (0)27 967 1812

Lifts/Pedestrian: in the Trockener Steg building.

A handy place to stop and eat if

you are skiing for a full day on this side. The food is fine but the atmosphere not particularly exciting. Good for a short lunch stop. Serves dishes such as fish, chicken curry and pork schnitzel as well as the usual salads and sandwiches.

Tufternalp (3)
T: +41 (0)27 967 5495

*Lifts: **Tuftern (9)** from top of Patrullarve chair (D), just before the wide piste turns into a path through the trees, the restaurant is on your left, Pedestrian: from Sunnegga, follow walking trail across to Tufternalp (25 minutes).*

Self-service restaurant serving a limited menu of homemade soup, cheese and sausage. Although a convenient pit stop, the service can sometimes be a little unfriendly.

Zum See (22)
T: +41 (0)27 967 2045

*Lifts: from Furi, ski halfway down **Blatten (50)**, look for sign on the right-hand side, Pedestrian: on walking path between town and Furi (25 minutes up from town, 15 minutes down from Furi), Food service: 12-5pm, evening meals for groups of 30 plus people can be arranged.*

Set amongst ancient barns (stadels), Zum See is one of Zermatt's most famous and favourite restaurants. A must-visit for any foodie; the cuisine, décor and situation will impress even the harshest critic. Dishes include lamb fillet, homemade pasta and their legendary Napolean (an amazing pastry and cream dessert). Half-portions are available although it's not the most child-friendly restaurant on the mountain. The restaurant is on the run back to town, making it perfect for a long late lunch, followed by a short ski home. A litre of house wine costs from 40chf.

Can't ski? Won't ski?
Too much snow or not
enough...?
Find out about **other
things to do** in Zermatt.

**What you'll find in
this chapter...**

The **map** on page 9 shows the
resort's main shopping areas.

For information on equipment hire
see page 42.

Gone are the days where all there was to do in a ski resort was to ski, eat, drink and ski again. Resorts are now providing alternative pastimes that don't involve hurtling down mountains on planks - although some do involve just as much adrenaline.

Zermatt is no exception, offering a huge number of diverse activities from tobogganing to ice climbing and hiking to paragliding. On snowshoes you can travel around the ski area seeing the spectacular panoramas and, if you're lucky, some of the local wildlife.

Or if kicking back and relaxing in a steam bath or floating around a tranquil swimming pool is more your idea of a holiday, then Zermatt also delivers.

Art and Exhibitions
The Alpine Museum
Bahnhofstrasse, next to the church on the main street,
www.zermatt.ch.
See page 131.

Vernissage
Hofmattstrasse 4, turn right out of the station, walk 100m and turn left - the cinema is on your right,
+41 (0)27 967 6636,
www.vernissage-zermatt.com.

Local artist Heinz Julen (page 13) exhibits his work and that of visiting artists in this trendy cinema.

Ask at the tourist office for information on current exhibitions.

Beauty, massage and spas
Beauty Life
Hotel Berghof, Winkelmattenweg 18, +41 (0)27 966 6900,
www.berghof-zermatt.ch.

A range of massages and beauty treatments available.

Daniela Steiner Spa

*Mont Cervin Palace, Bahnhofstrasse
31, opposite the Alpine Centre,
Tuesday to Sunday: 9am-8pm,
Monday: 2.30-8pm, +41 (0)27 966
8888,* www.seiler-hotels.ch.

Non-residents can use the spa
at the glorious 5-star Mont Cervin
Palace and it's definitely worth a
visit. The spa offers a huge range
of treatments from massages
(125chf for 50 minutes) to
pedicures and manicures (from
65chf) to a four hour package of
bliss including reflexology and
other treatments for 465chf.
Reservations essential.

Hotel Mirabeau Alpine Refuge

*Untere Mattenstrasse, turn left out
of the station and walk down the*

road; you will see Untere on your right, 9-11am, 2-9pm, treatments: 9am-9pm, swimming pool: 7am-9pm, +41 (0)27 966 2660, www.hotel-mirabeau.ch.

Luxurious range of treatments for men and women including pedicures (from 90chf) and whole body massages from 95chf for 50 minutes. They also offer treatment packages for couples for 170chf per person. Non-residents can use the swimming pool, sauna and the other spa facilities for 50chf in conjunction with a treatment. Alternatively, hire your own relaxation area for 35chf per person (from two to eight people).

Vanessa Beauty-Oase
Alpenhof Hotel, on the west bank of the river at the northern end of town, +41 (0)27 966 5555, www.alpenhofhotel.com.

Range of massages and beauty treatments.

Bowling, pool and table football
Country Bar
Hotel Elite, follow Hofmattstrasse down past the ice rink, the bar is on the right after the second crossroads, 10am-2am, +41 (0)27 967 1596, www.elite-zermatt.ch, 16chf per hour and table.

The Country Bar is tucked away under Hotel Elite. With five pool tables available, plus darts on offer, this is a good place to spend bad weather days.

Hotel Bristol
Schluhmattstrasse 3, follow Kirchstrasse down over the river and at the second road the hotel is on your right, +41 (0)27 966 3366, www.hotel-bristol.ch (German only).

Bowling, darts and table football.

Cinema
Vernissage
Hofmattstrasse 4, turn right out of the station, walk 100m and turn left - the cinema is on your right, 5pm-2am, +41 (0)27 967 6636, www.vernissage-zermatt.com, entry: 16chf.

Heinz Julen, a Zermatt artist and architect, designed this unique venue (see page 13). As well as being the local cinema, the

Vernissage has a bar (page 99) and lounge restaurant and hosts parties, club nights and exhibitions. As a cinema it shows all the most recent releases (some even before they are out in the UK). Most films are in English although you should arrive early as these are usually very popular.

Climbing
Triftbachhalle
Walk down Kirchstrasse and bear left before the park, carry on down this street and the hall is on your right, Monday: 9-10.30pm, Thursday: 7-10.30pm, Friday: 5.30-9pm and Saturday: 4-7pm.

The Triftbachhalle is a community hall where you can practice indoor climbing.

Alpine Centre
Bahnhofstrasse, 8.30am-12pm, 3-7pm, +41 (0)27 966 2460, www.alpincenter-zermatt.ch, from 80chf.

Book through the Alpine Centre for guided climbing in the Triftbachhalle on Monday, Thursday and Friday evenings.

Curling
Curling Club Zermatt
Obere Matten, turn right out of the train station, walk 100m and turn left and head down Hofmattstrasse until you see the ice rink on your left, +41 (0)27 966 3000, 8chf per person per hour.

Curling lessons are available on this floodlit ice-rink, or get a group together and just have a go.

Gorge Adventure
Alpine Centre

Bahnhofstrasse, 8.30am-12pm, 3-7pm, +41 (0)27 966 2460, www.alpincenter-zermatt.ch, 120chf for a group (four to seven people) or 450chf for a private lesson.

Take a guided climb through impressive rock formations that have been created by the rushing water below. Climb through a 1km passage which takes about three to four hours secured by rope and led by an experienced guide.

Helicopter rides
Air Zermatt

Spissstrasse 107, left out of the station and head to the end of town (about 500m), Air Zermatt is on your left, +41 (0)27 966 8686,

www.air-zermatt.ch (German only), 210chf for 20 minutes.

Sightseeing in a thrilling helicopter ride over the glaciers that surround Zermatt.

Horse-drawn carriages and sleighs
Werner Imboden

Either phone and book them to collect you somewhere (hotel/chalet) or they can often be picked up in the station square, +41 (0)79 436 7612, kutschen@bluewn.ch.

Sit back and enjoy the view as you are taken around town in style by horse-drawn carriage or, if there is enough snow, in a traditional horse-drawn sleigh.

Ice climbing
Alpine Centre

Bahnhofstrasse, 8.30am-12pm, 3-7pm, +41 (0)27 966 2460, www.alpincenter-zermatt.ch, 170chf for group (max four) or 470chf for a private lesson.

Learn to climb up various frozen waterfalls in and around Zermatt. Excursions for experienced climbers also available.

Ice skating

Obere Matten, turn right out of the train station, walk 100m and turn left and head down Hofmattstrasse until you see the ice rink on your left, +41 (0)27 967 3673.

Natural and artificial skating rink with toy penguins for children to hold on to for stability.

Igloo Village
Igloo-dorf
Rotenboden, take the Gornergrat train to Riffelberg Hotel where you'll be met and taken to the Igloo Village, +41 (0)41 612 2728, www.iglu-dorf.com, from 140chf per person per night.

Spend a unique night in your very own igloo up in the Gornergrat mountains. The price includes use of a whirlpool, a fondue dinner and breakfast the next day. To keep you warm, sheepskin and expedition sleeping bags are provided – along with the glühwein of course. Romantic packages (with prosecco and special food as wells as a 'romantic' igloo) are available as well as free-riding and snowshoeing packages. Advance booking is essential.

Internet access
Country Bar
Hotel Elite, follow Hofmattstrasse down past the ice rink, the bar is on the right after the second crossroads, 10am-2am, +41 (0)27 967 1596, www.elite-zermatt.ch, 6chf for half-an-hour, 12chf for one hour.

Some of the computers have word processing, printers and webcams as well as internet access.

Hotel Post
Bahnhofstrasse 41, 7am-2am, +41 (0)27 967 1931, www.hotelpost.ch, 1chf for five minutes or 12chf for one hour.

Pappererla Pub
Steinmattstrasse 34, walk over the bridge away from town on Kirchstrasse and you'll see the pub on your left, 2.30pm-2am, +41 (0)27 967 4040, www.papperlapub.ch.

Wireless internet plus a computer at the bar – both free.

Stoked Internet Corner
Hofmattstrasse 7, 8am-7pm, +41 (0)27 967 7020, www.stoked.ch, 7chf for half-an-hour, 20chf for two hours or longer, passes available.

Printing, copying, scanning, CD burner, hot spot, Ethernet connections.

Library
Bahnhofstrasse 92, 4-8pm, closed Wednesdays and weekends, +41 (0)27 967 5700.

Paragliding
Paragliding Zermatt
Haus Montana, Bachstrasse 8, on the river between Hofmattstrasse and Kirchstrasse, 8am-8pm, +41 (0)27 967 6744, www.paragliding-zermatt.ch, 150chf for a flight from Rothorn to Sunnegga, 190chf for Rothorn to town.

See Zermatt's stunning scenery from the skies and take in the view of the surrounding 4000m peaks as you glide above the mountains and ski trails below. A trained instructor will make sure you are relaxed and can fully enjoy the exhilarating flight.

Museum
Alpine Museum
Bahnhofstrasse, next to the church, www.zermatt.ch.

A newly-built museum in the middle of town. See the changes that took place to turn a small farming village into an internationally famous ski resort. Learn about the Matterhorn and the intrepid adventurers that climbed the magnificent mountains surrounding Zermatt. The museum has a section dedicated to Whymper's expedition to climb the Matterhorn as well as the rope involved in the controversial accident (page 10).

Climbers' graveyard

The small graveyard next to the church has tombstones dedicated to the many men and women who have lost their lives trying to climb the surrounding peaks. The furthest side of the graveyard has the memorial stones for those who died descending the Matterhorn after the famous conquering climb of 14 July 1865.

Sightseeing

Historical walking tours through the village are available with the following guides (12chf per person with a minimum of four people):

Edith Villiger-Imark

T: +41 (0)27 967 2900
E: e-villiger@bluewin.ch.

Elisabeth Fux

T: +41 (0)27 967 3613
    (0)79 332 80 34
W: www.fuxelisabeth@bluewin.ch

Visit the Peaks

T: +41 (0)27 966 0101

W: www.matterhornparadise.ch
Click on 'rates' on the left-hand side, Peak Pass for three days: 168chf (adult), 84chf (child 6-16yrs), free for children under six years.

Start at any of the three main lift stations in town: Sunnegga, Gornergrat or Klein Matterhorn. Visit Rothorn's spectacular views of 37 peaks over 4000m surrounding Zermatt; touch the Matterhorn at Schwarzsee or ascend to the Klein Matterhorn, the highest sightseeing point in Europe.

Glacier Palace

Take the cable cars from the Klein Matterhorn lift station up to the top of Klein Matterhorn. Walk out of the lift station and the Glacier Palace is in front of you, 9am-3.45pm. Klein

Matterhorn return: 82chf (adult), 41chf (child 9-16yrs), free for children under nine. Entry to Glacier Paradise is free.

Situated at 3820m and 15m under glacier ice, the Glacier Paradise houses some stunning ice sculptures as well as huge natural ice crystals formed from the ceiling. Look into a natural crevasse and learn about the glacier.

Glacier Express

T: +41 (0)27 927 7777
W: www.glacierexpress.ch
From 129chf for an adult ticket, children under six travel free, six - 16 year olds travel half price. If you're after a longer sightseeing trip, take the Glacier Express from Zermatt to St. Moritz. The journey takes seven-and-a-half hours, crosses 291 bridges and travels through 91 tunnels. With a dining car and bar on board, you can relax as you take in the stunning Alpine scenery.

Snowshoeing and Hiking

Venture into the mountains and explore the Alpine forests, take in the breathtaking scenery and spot some of the local wildlife. Equipped with snowshoes and poles, you can follow any of Zermatt's five marked trails made up of over 45km of routes. Snowshoes are available to rent from hire shops and cost around 15chf per day. Or you can just hike with appropriate footwear. Collect a hiking map from the tourist office.

Hiking is free unless you choose to use the lift system to get you higher into the mountains (although you may then need to take snowshoes). Otherwise take one of the paths signposted for the resort.

To use the lifts, the Peak Pass - designed for hiking and snowshoeing - is available from the lift pass offices (page 33). Peak Pass for three days: 168chf (adult), 84chf (child six-16 years), free for children under six years old.

You may choose to take a guided tour and learn about your surroundings as you hike. The Alpine Centre (+41 (0)27 966 2460, www.alpincenter-zermatt.ch) does group tours (four to seven people) for 130chf or private tours for 450chf.

Swimming pools
The Arca salt-water swimming pool

Hotel Arca, Spissstrasse 42, turn left out of the train station and follow the street, the hotel is on your right, 9am-4pm, 7-9.30pm for non-residents, +41 (0)27 967 1544, www.arca-zermatt.ch.

Massage jets and Roman steam baths. Children are not allowed into the swimming pool.

Hotel Christiania

Weististrasse 7, take Sunneggastrasse from the river at the northern end of town and take the second left, 8-10.30am, 2-8pm, Tuesday: 2-8pm, Thursday: 8-10.30am, +41 (0)27 966 8000, www.christiania-zermatt.com, 10chf (adult) or 6chf (children). Alternatively, get 10 entries for 90chf (a 10% discount). Sauna and swim: 20chf, gym: 6chf.

This hotel has a large heated indoor swimming pool (25m x 12m), a sauna and a gym.

Hotel Eden

Reidstrasse 5, follow Kirchstrasse down and walk over the river and keep going and the hotel is on your left, 9am-4pm, +41 (0)27 967 2655, www.hotel-eden.ch .

This hotel has an adventure indoor swimming pool. Children need to be accompanied by an adult.

Hotel Silvana

Furi, accessed by the Klein Matterhorn lift, 7am-4pm, +41 (0)27 966 2800, www.zermatt.ch/silvana.

Indoor swimming pool

(12x8m) and jacuzzi, sauna and steam bath from 4-7pm. Children are admitted if they're accompanied by an adult.

Style Hotel
Untere Mattenstrasse 50, turn left out of the station and walk until Untere is on your right, turn right and walk for 100m, open until 5pm, 7-9pm, +41 (0)27 966 5666, www.stylehotel.ch.

A 13 x 7.5m pool in a spa-like atmosphere with loungers resting in the shallow water to relax on. The jacuzzi is a good size too.

Tobogganing

There are three approved toboggan runs in Zermatt (tobogganing on the ski runs is too dangerous).

Most ski hire shops rent sledges for about 15chf per day.

Rotenboden to Riffelberg
Take the Gornergrat train to Rotenboden, 8am-5pm, +41 (0)27 921 4111, www.gornergrat.ch, use your ski pass (page 33).

Rent your toboggan at Rotenboden and sledge down the track 1.5km to Riffelberg. Then jump back on the train and do it all again! Take care until you get used to it as the track can be pretty fast in places.

Sunnegga
Every Wednesday (mid-December to mid-April) you can have dinner at Restaurant Sunnegga and then toboggan back to town (or take the cable car if you've eaten too

much!). To reserve call Restaurant Sunnegga (page 121) before 3pm. The one-way train ride and fondue costs from 33chf.

Furi
Every Thursday (December to March) from 7.30pm you can join in the toboggan fun ride from Furi to Zermatt.

Contact the tourist office for more details.

Trampolines
Vincent Hueber
Near the ice rink on Hofmattstrasse, open daily in the afternoons and mornings at peak times, +41 (0)79 214 3270, www.zermatt-fun.ch. 10chf for around seven minutes per person.

Video/DVD Hire
DVD Rental
In the Viktoria Center, opposite Coop, +41 (0)27 968 1800.

Tourists can rent English DVDs for 8chf per night, leaving credit card details as a deposit.

Shopping
The main drag is Zermatt's prime shopping street, although there are some real gems to be found (sometimes quite literally) in the alleys and roads branching off from here. There are a multitude of shops selling gemstones, different types of jewellery, watches and Swiss army knives so it's treats and presents galore if you have the money. Or, if you prefer, you can shop endlessly for equipment and ski clothes in the many sports outlets. We've only listed a couple of the more interesting ones here, as we recommend you spend time browsing.

Opening hours
Unless otherwise stated, most shops are open from early morning until early evening. Quite a few close for a couple of hours over lunchtime (although this can sometimes change at weekends, especially at peak times). Hours can vary so if it's essential, phone ahead to check.

Equipment and clothes
Anorak
Bahnhofstrasse 20, 8.30am-12pm, 2-7pm, +41 (0)27 968 1777, www.anorak-zermatt.ch.

A high-quality shop for different types of mountain gear that also hires out a range of telemarking and touring equipment. Stocks brands such as Patagonia, Norrona, Scarpa and Black Diamond. Head here if you are after specialist equipment.

Peak Performance

Bahnhofstrasse 20, 9am-12.30pm, 2.30-7.30pm, +41 (0)27 967 24 91, peak_zermatt@bluewin.ch.

A huge Peak Performance shop with everything you could want.

Stoked Street Wear Store

Hofmattstrasse 7, next to the floodlit ice rink, Tuesday to Saturday: 8.30am-12pm, 2-6.30pm, Mondays: open until 7pm, +41 (0)27 967 1133, www.stoked.ch.

Impressive selection of streetwear from popular brands such as Burton, Etnies and Nikita. Has everything from shoes, belts, hats and goggles to full ski/snowboard outfits to kit you out for the slopes.

Check out page 45 for more shops that sell ski clothing and equipment.

Food and wine
Coop

In the Viktoria Centre, opposite the train station, Monday to Saturday: 8.30am-7pm, Sunday: open only in the afternoon.

A large supermarket with a good selection of produce including a range of sandwiches and salads. Delivery service available.

Josi cheese and wine

Tempel 9, behind the Alpine Centre, 9am-12pm, 3-7pm, +41 (0)27 966 2430, www.cheese-

wine.ch (German only).

A great selection of local and international cheese and wine. Try the local Zermatter Mütschli cheese.

Migros
Hofmattstrasse, Sunday to Friday: 8.30am-12pm, 2-6.30pm, Saturday: only open until 6pm, +41 (0)27 967 3181.

This supermarket also has a large selection of produce but does not sell alcohol. As in most ski resorts, prices are higher than down the mountain.

Welschen Wines
Spissstrasse 26 & Hofmattstrasse 14, +41 (0)27 967 2222, www.weinewelschen.ch

Founded in 1964, this wine shop sells speciality wines as well as beer, mineral water and spirits.

Butchers
Bayard Willy
Bahnhofstrasse, 8am-12pm, 2-7pm, +41 (0)27 967 2266, www.metzgerei-bayard.ch (German only).

A great butcher that also sells an impressive selection of local produce such as wine, pasta and delicatessen products.

Zuber Gottfried
Spissstrasse, +41 (0)27 967 3936.

Bakeries
The bakeries all sell pretty much

the same thing; a good selection of freshly baked bread, pastries and sandwiches, as well as some milk, cheese and eggs. Try the Valais specialties of Zermatter Baumnusstorte (cake with nuts) or Shoko Matterhorn (chocolate).

Biner
Uferweg 1, Kirchplatz 18, Bahnhofplatz 23, +41 (0)27 967 6167, www.biner.ch (German only).
Fuchs
Bahnhofstrasse 72, +41 (0)27 967 2212.

Kirchstrasse 46, +41 (0)27 967 5960.

Getwingstrasse 24, +41 (0)27 967 2063.

Hörnli

Bahnhofstrasse 28, +41 (0)27 967 4457.

Zellner

Bahnhofstrasse, +41 (0)27 967 1855.

Chocolate and sweets shops

Merkur

Bahnhofstrasse, Monday to Saturday 9am-12pm, 2-7pm, Sunday 4-7pm, +41 (0)27 967 4373, www.merkur.ch.

A dream shop for anyone with a sweet tooth. Plenty of boxed Swiss chocolates to choose from as well as tablets of homemade goodies, such as white chocolate with raspberries, dark chocolate with hazelnuts, and more. Even their window display is mouth-watering.

Newsagents and tobacconists

Kkiosk

Bahnhofplatz, next to the station, Monday to Saturday: 7am-6.30pm, Sunday: 8am-6.30pm.
Also:
Just off Bahnhofstrasse, next to UBS, Monday to Friday: 8am-12.30pm, 1.30-6.30pm, Saturday: 8am-12.30pm, 1.30-6pm, closed Sundays.

Both outlets sell magazines, cigarettes, newspapers, souvenirs, postcards and phone cards.

Hardware shop

Aufdenblatten & Co.

Hofmattstrasse 14, +41 (0)27 967 5723.

General hardware store.

Bahnhofstrasse 5,
+41 (0)27 967 3433.
aufco.eisenwaren@swissonline.ch.

Plenty of things for your kitchen. If you are planning on buying some Swiss kitchen knives or a fondue set, this is the place to come.

Pharmacies

Apotheke Testa Grigia

Bahnhofstrasse 21, 8.30am-12pm, 2-6.30pm, +41 (0)27 966 4949, testagrigiapharma@bluewin.ch.

Internationale Apotheke

Bahnhofstrasse 17, 08.30am-12pm, 2-6.30pm, +41 (0)27 966 2727, info@pharmazermatt.ch.

Photography
Alpine Photo Shop

Chalet Albert, Bahnhofstrasse 4, 8am-12pm, 2-7pm closed Sundays, +41 (0)27 967 5588, www.alpinephotoshop.com.

This shop has a great selection of Zermatt photographs, postcards, and souvenirs as well as being a good place to get your holiday snaps developed.

Foto-Fast

Bahnhofplatz, +41 (0)27 967 4400.

Zermatt photographs, postcards and souvenirs as well as photo developing.

Other shopping
Bucherer

Bahnhofstrasse 6, 8.30am-12pm, 2-6.30pm, +41 (0)27 967 5353, www.bucherer.com.

One of the most luxurious and therefore expensive jewellery and watch shops in Zermatt. Selling brands such as Rolex, Gucci and TAGHeuer, it's worth going in for a browse.

Swatch

Bahnhofstrasse, opposite UBS bank, 8.30am-12pm, 2-6.30pm,

+41 (0)27 967 8067, swatch.zermatt@rhone.ch.

A store entirely devoted to Swatch watches. Particularly popular in Zermatt as you can have your lift pass loaded onto a special Swatch watch (…only in Switzerland!).

Wega

Bahnhohplatz 6, 8.30am-12pm, 2-7pm, +41 (0)27 967 2166, www.wega-zermatt.ch. Two other shops on the main street.

Every Swiss or Zermatt souvenir you could want, from Swiss army knives to St. Bernard cuddly toys. You're bound to find something to take home.

Skiing with **children**... dream or nightmare? With a little planning, it can be your best ski holiday ever. Read this chapter for the low down.

With its extreme mountains and high altitudes, at first glance Zermatt doesn't appear to be a particularly child-friendly resort. There are no baby slopes in the town, nor the large choice of childcare provisions that you find in other resorts. However, with free lift passes for under nines and half-price passes for under 16s, Zermatt can be a canny choice for those with children who can already ski.

The majority of tour operators here offer very little in the way of their own childcare. However, using the contacts given in this chapter, you should find everything you might need on a family holiday from evening babysitters to full day crèches.

For the little ones, there is the large and lively crèche, Kinderparadies (page 145) as well as other smaller crèches in hotels that can be used by non-residents. Once children start to get a bit too old for ball ponds and slides, Stoked's Snowflakes Kids' Club (page 145 and page 147) in Schwarzsee has a fun park for children to learn the basics of skiing from the age of four up to 12. Once they're ready to start learning properly, ski schools such as Summit run lessons for kids (page 148). Zermatt also thoughtfully provides ski lockers at the base lift stations so that you don't have to carry your children's skis around town for them.

In this chapter, we have listed a choice of services on offer, all of which you will need to book in advance. We also list those companies or hotels who have special facilities for kids. For up-to-date information on family accommodation options, check out our website: **maddogski.com**.

Accommodation

With only a couple of tour operators offering their own childcare in Zermatt, the hotels seem to be a better option, with the entire Seiler group (page 144) as well as some independents, such as Hotel Ginabelle (page 144) offering free childcare for guests – some hotels include childcare costs in your room rate.

All the accommodation options have pros and cons. Children love the social environment of hotels and chalets. However self-catering allows you complete flexibility, especially when it comes to mealtimes. If you have young children, it may be better to stay close to a bus stop although there are taxis available to take you around in Zermatt (page 162).

Children's checklist

When booking your holiday, there are a number of questions you may want to ask:

- Are there price reductions available for children?
- Are paraphernalia like cots, high chairs, children's cutlery, buggies and baby monitors provided? If not, can they be bought/hired nearby?
- Does the company offer a nappy-buying service or will you have to bring/buy your own?
- Can extra beds be added into the parents' room?
- Are any other children booked into the chalet? How old are they?
- Are the children's rooms located away from communal areas (which can be noisy until late)?

- Are there baths available (some accommodation only has showers)?
- Have they had complaints in the past about sound proofing in the bedrooms? Quite a few people comment on this and it can be stressful being kept awake by children in the next door room - or feeling guilty about keeping everyone else up.
- Does the company provide its own nannies and/or babysitters? What qualifications do they have and what is the adult to child ratio?
- If childcare isn't provided, can they recommend local carers/facilities?
- Can the company pre-book ski school?

- Can high tea be arranged for children? Are they given different food?
- Is it a long walk to the lifts/nearest bus stop? If so, does the company provide transport?

Child-friendly tour operators

Whilst few companies have their own childcare provision, these tour operators are well-known for their focus on families and offer their own programmes. Other operators may offer free child places or discounted or free equipment hire. Check out **maddogski.com** for up to date information.

Crystal
T: +44 (0)870 160 6040
W: www.crystalski.co.uk.

Free equipment hire for children when both parents pre-book theirs.

Powder Byrne
T: +44 (0)208 246 5300
W: www.powderbyrne.com.

Runs a crèche for children aged from six months to three years. There are also various clubs available during the February half-term and Easter holidays - a Yeti Club for four to nine year olds, SnoZone or Boardzone for 10-14 year olds and a variety of skiing or boarding clinics available for teenagers.

Scott Dunn
T: +44 (0)208 682 5050
W: www.scottdunn.com/ski.

143

Childcare for kids aged six months to 13 years with private nannies who will come to your chalet and pick older children up from ski school. They also thoughtfully stock nappies and wipes to save you packing them and provide an end of day report on your child's activities.

Hotels
Hotel Ginabelle
Vispastrasse 52, +41 (0)27 966 5000, www.la.ginabelle.ch.

A weekly childcare programme for guests (9am-10pm) and non-guests (9am-5pm) in the Pumuckel Club (page 145). The hotel can supply a whole range of baby equipment such as baths, listening phones and more.

Seiler Hotels
Nicoletta, Mont Cervin Palace, Monte Rosa, Schweizerhof & Résidence, Riffelalp Resort, www.seilerhotels.ch.

The Nicoletta Hotel provides the Nico Kids' Club free for all Seiler Hotels' guests from 9am-5.30pm.

Lift passes
Zermatt Mountain Cableways offers free lift passes to children under nine years old and half-price passes to those under 16. See www.matterhornparadise.ch for more information.

We have included a summary of the prices for chilren and teenagers here.

Lift pass prices (chf) (high season): Zermatt pass

No of days	Child (9-15)	Youth (16-20)
Half day	26	44
1	34	58
5	145	247
6	168	286
10	249	422
Season	683	1160

Cervinia: add on 37/day

For adult and senior lift pass prices, see On the piste, page 35.

Childcare

This is a selection of the crèches that are open to the public in Zermatt. As with all the services in this chapter, it is important that you book your child's place in advance – especially at peak times.

Kinderparadies

Spissstrasse 23, turn left out of the station and walk 200m, 9am-5pm, +41 (0)27 967 7252, www.kinderparadies-zermatt.ch.

Kinderparadies is a children's playground with ball ponds, Lego, activities and games galore for children from three months up to seven years old. A half day costs from 60chf and a full day from 110chf, with discounts if you book for a week.

Pumuckel Club

Hotel Ginabelle, Vispastrasse 52, 9am-5pm, +41 (0)27 966 5000, www.la.ginabelle.ch.

A weekly childcare programme open to the public that caters for children over two years old: dressing up, painting pictures and sledging as well as a welcome drink for the parents and children. The club will also organise midday meals and can provide babysitters for children under two years old.

Snowflakes Kids' Club

Stoked, Hofmattstrasse 7, 9am-3.30pm, +41 (0)27 967 7020, www.stoked.ch.

Situated at the top of the Schwarzsee ski area is a large childcare centre fitted with a rolling carpet and obstacles so that children can learn to ski on the flat, snowplough and learn to stop. Qualified childcare specialists look after children from three years of age. Prices range from 25chf for one hour to 445chf for five whole days.

Babysitters

These are all self-employed private babysitters so it's important that you check the qualifications yourself of any private babysitters.

Breda Amalia

Haus Brunnmatt,
+41 (0)27 967 2606.
English spoken.

Ferreira-Wyden Christine

Haus Everest, Schluhmattstrasse 27, +41 (0)27 967 0137.
Looks after children of all ages daytime and evenings. English spoken.

Kaufmann Jasmin

Chalet Chouca, Zer Bännu 7, +41 (0)27 967 4931.
Takes children from one month to 10 years both daytimes and evenings. English spoken.

Ruetsch Irene

Chalet Arvenhof, Hofmattstrasse 3, +41 (0)27 967 4931.
Looks after children of all ages daytime and evenings. English spoken.

Ski school

Generally, children can start skiing from around aged four. The stronger they are, the easier it is for them and the more fun they will have, so although starting younger is possible, older may be preferable. Very young children (aged three to six) may only have the energy to do half a day on the slopes so the rest of the day might be better spent playing in the snow, or back in the resort (see suggested activities on page 149).

Many instructors teach children to ski through a series of games, analogies, copying and races, so they pick up new skills without too much technical information. Kids may come home talking about how they were making 'chips' and not 'pizza' – this just means that they are moving into parallels instead of snowplough – or being 'tall as a house' and 'small as a mouse', which is a useful way to encourage children to move up at the start of the turn and down at the end.

Skiing is all about having fun, so don't worry too much about the progress of very young children. If your child is having a good time, they'll be hooked for life and the technical improvement will come. If you have any worries, speak to the instructor.

Groups vs private lessons

It used to be that in order for children to get the individual attention they need to progress technically, private lessons were the only option. However, ski schools now offer smaller group sizes for children (between five and 10 members) where the children can enjoy the social side of being in a class but still receive individual instruction. Kids love the interaction with other children that groups offer, so this can be the ideal environment to learn in. With encouragement and friendly competition, many children progress very quickly.

Ski school for children gets very booked up in Zermatt so it is important to book in advance if you are visiting over UK school holidays. Every year, people are disappointed that they can't get their kids into ski school. Before booking, check that your accommodation provider doesn't have discounts with any of the schools.

When booking, check that your child will have an English-speaking instructor as not all the schools offer this. Also, it's worth asking where the meeting point for lessons is (especially if you are taking lessons as well) so that you can be on hand to drop off and collect your kids. For full details of all the schools see page 38.

Snowflakes Kids' Club

Stoked, Hofmattstrasse 7, +41 (0)27 967 7020, www.stoked.ch.

For four to 12 year olds at Schwarzsee Paradise, there are different groups for each level of competence. Maximum group size of eight children. Lessons start on a Monday and you can book five full days (10am-3pm) for 445chf.

Summit Ski and Snowboard School

Perren Reinhold Sport, Bahnhofstrasse, +41 (0)27 967 0001, www.summitskischool.com.

Summit has a kids' club for six to 10 year olds of all levels and an advanced group, 'New Schoolers', which runs for 10 to 15 year olds. All the kids' groups are taught in English and there are a maximum of six children in each group. Starting on a Sunday, six full days (9.30am-3.30pm) costs 550chf.

The Swiss Ski & Snowboard School

Alpine Centre, Bahnhofstrasse,

+41 (0)27 966 2466, www.skischulezermatt.ch.

Four to five year olds go to the Snowli Kids' Village up at Riffelberg, five full days (10am-3pm) costs 385chf. Children's ski school is available for six to 12 year olds where they can join levels one to five according to the Swiss Snow League system. The kids meet at 9am and classes end at 3.30pm. Five full days costs 340chf.

First day at ski school checklist

- Write your mobile or other contact number on a piece of paper and place it in your child's coat pocket in case you are needed urgently
- Plenty of high factor sun cream

(water resistant and at least 30 SPF) is essential. Put the tube in their pocket so they can top up throughout the day
- Most experts recommend that children should ski with helmets (in Italy it is a legal requirement). You can hire these in resort
- Younger eyes are more sensitive so it is important to make kids wear good quality sunglasses or goggles all the time. If you only plan to buy one or the other, buy goggles
- Take time to find gloves or mittens that your child can take on and off easily by themselves; they'll have to do this numerous times throughout the day!
- A small rucksack is useful for older kids for carrying drinks,

snacks and sun cream
- Children lose body heat faster than adults – make sure they are wrapped up warmly
- If you are booking younger children into ski school, remember to give them a drink and snack for the mid-lesson break (or money to buy them). Check with the ski school if you are unsure
- Talk to the instructor before the first lesson as any information will be useful (for example, do they get tired easily/hate drag lifts/have any allergies or other medical considerations)
- Even if your children are not in ski school, you will probably find it helpful to mark clothes, skis and helmets with their name as

things are often thrown into a big bundle in the rush to get inside at break or lunch time! If you don't have any labels for skis and helmets, write on sticking plasters
- If possible buy gloves and hats that can be attached to your child or their jacket; otherwise they go missing endlessly...
- Complete beginners (especially the little ones) will probably not need to take poles to their ski lessons, at least for the first few days – check with your ski school

Children's activities
Many of the suggestions in **Other things to do** (page 125) are also suitable for children. We have listed the most relevant ones below.

Ice skating
Obere Matten, +41 (0)27 967 3673.
Skating rink with toy penguins for children to hold onto for stability (page 129).

Swimming
Hotel Christiania, Weististrasse 7, +41 (0)27 966 8000.
Large heated swimming pool (page 134).

Tobogganing
Rotenboden to Riffelberg, +41 (0)27 921 4711.
Sledge 1.5km from Rotenboden to Riffelberg (page 135).

Restaurants

Most restaurants in Zermatt welcome children and provide either children's menus or half portions at discounted prices. Thanks to the type of food local to Zermatt, it's easy to get simple pasta dishes, pizzas or rösti tailored to suit your child's likes and dislikes. Our restaurant reviews (page 83) have more detailed write-ups but we particularly recommend these places.

Old Spaghetti Factory
T: +41 (0)27 967 1931.

A fun and lively restaurant with a huge menu and something to please everyone, young and old (page 87).

Pizzeria Broken
T: +41 (0)27 967 1931

Part of the Hotel Post complex, kids will love this pizzeria where they can create their own pizzas (page 89).

Restaurant Stockhorn
T: +41 (0)27 967 1747

A good value grill restaurant that is perfect for taking the children to try some traditional Alpine food. Cheese fondues and raclettes make for an entertaining meal for older children (page 90).

Walliserkanne
T: +41 (0)27 966 4610

A mid-priced place for families and big groups, the Walliserkanne is a lively and busy restaurant with a varied menu (page 91).

Mountain restaurants

Many mountain restaurants are suitable for children and we've included reviews of all mountain restaurants in the ski area (page 100) but these are our favourites if you have little ones with you. Some are accessible for non-skiers but we've also included a few gems that are on easier runs.

Chez Vrony
T: +41 (0)27 967 2552

A special atmosphere and a good place to take children; as well as the variety of dishes on offer, kids are given crayons. Children's choices on the menu range from 8-14 chf (page 109).

Findlerhof – Franz & Heidi
T: +41 (0)27 967 2588

One for the families that prefer gastronomic excellence to basic easy fare (page 110).

Pizzeria Cervino
T: +41 (0)27 967 1812

The pizzas are excellent and small portions are available for children although a small pizza doesn't cost much less than standard one (page 118).

Riffelberg Self-Service Restaurant
T: +41 (0)27 966 6500

A large and busy restaurant that serves well as a quick and cheap lunch stop (page 119).

Restaurant Rothorn
T: +41 (0)27 967 2675

A child-friendly restaurant that is also pleasant for adults and has a welcoming atmosphere and reasonable food (page 120).

Restaurant Sunnegga
T: +41 (0)27 967 3046

Busy but spacious restaurant that is easily accessible for skiers of all standards, making it a good place to meet up with beginners and non-skiers (page 121).

Papermoon

Bahnhofstrasse 60, next to the Alpine Centre, 9am-12pm, 3-6pm, +41 (0)27 967 22 02.

Children's clothing store that sells great kids' ski suits by brands such as SOS, Peak Performance, O'Neill and Diesel.

Boutique Niki

Hofmattstrasse, walk 100m from the station up main street and turn left, shop is about 10m up on the left-hand side, 9am-12pm, 3-6pm.

Upmaket fashion outlet selling brands including Burberry, Timberland and DKNY.

Shopping

Supermarkets in Zermatt have a wide choice of products including baby food and formula but if you have any favourite products it's best to bring them with you. Most ski shops stock children's sizes and there are plenty of clothing shops so it's easy to replace any lost items. We have listed a few child-specific clothing shops here.

The list — sounds boring but it has all the important information that you don't need till you need it...

- Telephone numbers include the international dialling code. From Zermatt, drop the '+41' and then dial the number using the (0)

- Swiss mobile numbers begin with '07'

- We use local landmarks and main streets as points of reference. Locations of these are shown in detail on page 9

- You can pick up an *Ortsplan* (village map) from the tourist office

Banks, bureau de change and cashpoints

There are numerous banks located along the main street, all of which have cashpoints. Opening hours are Monday to Friday unless specified.

Credit Suisse

Bahnhofstrasse 57, 9am-12pm, 3-6pm, +41 (0)27 966 3266.

Raiffeisenbank

Bahnhofstrasse 26, 8.30am-12pm, 2.30-6pm, +41 (0)27 966 6960. Additional cashpoint at the bottom of the Matterhorn Express.

UBS AG

Bahnhofstrasse 29, 9am-12pm, 3-6pm, +41 (0)27 966 9811. The cashpoint here offers the option of euros as well as Swiss francs.

Walliser Kantonalbank

Bahnhofstrasse, near the Alpine Centre, 9am-12pm, 2-5.30pm, +41 (0)27 966 9700.

Bureau de change
Change 4U

Bahnhofplatz, 8.30am-12pm, 2-6.30pm, open Saturdays, +41 (0)27 967 7770, www.change4u.ch.

Buses

Zermatt has electrically-powered buses that run on two routes (green and red) throughout the town, stopping at all the major intersections. Stops are shown by red dots on the tourist office's village map and timetables are posted at the stops. The green bus is the most commonly used by visitors as it links up all three lift stations. The red route goes through the town as well but has a longer journey up through Winkelmatten at the southern end of town.

The bus is free with your ski pass so keep it with you when you change out of your ski clothes. If you don't have a ski pass you can pay (3/4chf). They also have special week passes available.

The buses can get crowded, especially at peak times so if you don't fancy taking a bus, then try one of the electro taxi services (page 162).

Car hire

Avis

Garage Christophe, Täsch,
+41 (0)27 967 3535,
www.garagechristophe.ch.

Hertz

Alphubel Taxi Parking, Täsch, +41
(0)27 967 4549, www.alphubel.ch.

For information on car hire from
airports, see page 21. Zermatt is a
car-free resort so you can only
drive as far as Täsch where you will
need to park and then take the
train (page 163) the rest of the way.

Car parks

Matterhorn Terminal

Täsch, +41 (0)27 967 1214,
www.matterhornterminal.ch.

A huge new car park in Täsch with
2100 covered car parking spaces.
Attached to the Täsch to Zermatt
train station, car parking costs
11chf per day or 77chf per week.
You can pay at machines in the
terminal and in the car park itself.

There are a number of
garages on the left-hand side as
you drive into Täsch that operate
car parks and taxi services (page
162)

Car repair

See car hire (page 21) for garages
in Täsch that can repair any
problems.

Cashpoints

See banks page 153.

Churches

**The Roman Catholic parish
church**

Bahnhofstrasse, +41 (0)27 967
2314.

St. Peter's – The English Church

Next to the post office, +41 (0)27
967 5566.

During the winter, the church
is open for visitors. Services are
held in English.

Cinema

Vernissage

Hofmattstrasse 4, turn right out of
the station, walk 100m and turn
left - the cinema is on your right,
5pm-2am, +41 (0)27 967 6636,
www.vernissage-zermatt.com,
entry 16chf.

Consulate

The consulate in Geneva is responsible for the canton of Valais (Zermatt) and Geneva. For lost passports in these places, contact the British Consulate in Geneva. You may then be referred to the Bern consulate.

British Consulate - Geneva
37-39 Rue de Vermont, Geneva, +41 (0)22 918 2400.

British Consulate - Bern
Thunstrasse 50, Bern, +41 (0)31 359 7700.

Credit cards

Credit cards are commonplace although many Zermatt businesses do not accept American Express.

When using your debit or credit card, you will normally need your PIN number.

Dentist (*Zahnärzt*)
Andreas Gottschalk
Haus Turuwang, Bahnhofplatz 58, +41 (0)27 967 8088, www.zahnarzt-zermatt.ch.

Hermann Steffen
Haus Venus, Steinmattstrasse 43, +41 (0)27 967 3467.

Doctor (*Ärzte*)
For skiing or emergency injuries, each doctor's office takes it in turn to be on-call. Telephone any of them to find out which it is that day.

Dr. med. Bannwart
Viktoria Center, Bahnhofplatz 6, +41 (0)27 967 1188.

Dr. med. Bieler-Hischier
Haus Pasadena, Getwingstrasse 30, +41 (0)27 967 4477.

Dr. med. Brönnimann
Haus Monazit, Schluhmattstrasse 15, +41 (0)27 967 1916.

Dr. med. Julen
Haus Magnolia, Bachstrasse 72, +41 (0)27 967 6717.

Dr med. Stoessel
Tempelareal, Bahnhofstrasse 50, +41 (0)27 967 7979.

Dogs

There are regulations in Zermatt if you have a dog:

- All dogs must be kept on a lead in the village
- Potentially dangerous dogs should be kept on lead at all times and wear a muzzle
- Owners must pick up their dog's mess
- Dogs aren't allowed in certain areas such as playgrounds

Dog sitting available from:

Breda Dorothe

Haus Bergamo, Kirchstrasse 16, +41 (0)27 967 6158.

Dry cleaners

See page 159.

Electricity

Switzerland operates on a 220 volts system and UK appliances should work with an adapter (the two round pin type).

Emergency numbers

The three digit numbers can only be called from Swiss mobiles or landlines so we have also included a number to call from UK mobiles.

Police: 117 or +41 (0)27 966 6920

Emergency services: 144 or +41 (0)333 333 333

Piste security: +41 (0)27 966 0101

Avalanche report: 187 or +41 (0)848 800 187

Breakdown and accident recovery service: +41 (0)27 966 3535

Events

A monthly events guide *(Veranstalungen/animations)* is available from the tourist office.

Environment

See Rubbish (page 161).

Hairdresser (*Friseur*)

Inter Coiffure Creative Team

Marco Stöckli, Seilerhaus, opposite Mont Cervin Palace, +41 (0)27 967 6644, www.creativeteam.ch.

Health

A few tips to keep you healthy on holiday:

- The sun is much stronger at altitude – make sure you wear a high SPF sun cream, even on overcast days
- You need to drink at least three

The environment

There is always a tremendous amount of rubbish on the slopes when the snow melts – don't add to it! A single cigarette butt contains 4,000 toxic substances and can pollute up to 1.3 m_ of snow – under any one chairlift there could be up to 30,000 butts.

How long does rubbish last?
Plastic bottle: 100 - 1000 years
Aluminium cans: 100 - 500 years
Cigarette stubs: 2 - 7 years
Fruit peel: 3 days - 6 months
Sweet wrappers: 100 - 450 years

Source: www.mountain-riders.org (French only)

The Ski Club of Great Britain is running a campaign to safeguard the environment and the long-term future of skiing. See **www.respectthemountain.com** for details.

times as much water to keep hydrated at altitude – more if you are topping up with wine and beer! Your muscles are the first part of your body to dehydrate so you'll suffer less aches and pains if you keep hydrated

- Good sunglasses are a must to prevent watering eyes and snow blindness
- Lip salve with a high sun-protection factor will prevent unattractive chapped lips!
- Prevention is better than cure – take the time to do at least a few stretches before and after skiing.

Hospital
Spitalzentrum Oberwallis
+41 (0)27 970 3333.
Visp: Pflanzettastrasse 8
Brig: Überlandstrasse 14

Information

The local Zermatt television channel provides current information such as weather, events, photos, documentary films and foreign news.

Internet

See page 130.

Language

Although many of the people working in shops and restaurants speak English, a little German goes a long way. Don't be discouraged if you don't understand their response as the Valais dialect is different to standard German.

Notes on the language:

- Nouns in German all start with a capital letter eg Fahrplan (bus timetable)

Useful words and phrases:	
Hello	Guten Tag
Good Morning	Guten Morgen
Goodbye	Auf Wiedersehen
How are you?	Wie geht's dir? (informal) Wie geht es Ihnen? (polite)
Please	Bitte
Thank you	Dankeschön/Vielen Danke
Excuse me/sorry	Entschuldigen Sie bitte
How much..?	Wieviel kostet…?
The bill please	Die Rechnung bitte
Jug of tap water	Einen Krug des Leitungswassers
Snowboard	Snowboard
Skis	Ski
Binding	Bindung
Ski /boarding boots	Skischuhe/Snowboard Schuhe
Ski poles	Stöcke
Lift pass	Skipass/Liftpass
I am lost	Ich bin verloren
Where is the nearest lift?/bar?	Wo ist die näheste Bergbahn? Kneipe?
Help!	Hilfe!
Watch out!	Vorsicht!

- Nouns also start with either der (m), die (f) or das (n) to signify gender. Plurals always begin with die. This is the equivalent of using 'the' in English
- When communicating there is a difference in 'you' to show the relationship between people. Either refer to Sie, the polite form, to people of authority, waiters, bank, etc, or Du, the informal version, used by friends and family
- German is quite easy to read since there are many similar sounds as in English. However, you will come across certain vowels that carry two dots above them, the umlaut, that signifies a joining of the letter 'e' and a different sound. They are pronounced in the following way:

- Ä (ae) – sounds like 'air' eg Äpfel (apples); Ü (ue) – sounds like 'oo' eg glück (luck); Ö (oe) - sounds like 'ur' eg schön (beautiful). Note: you can replace the umlaut with the letter 'e' eg Aepfel. This is considered just as correct
- People generally refer to themselves by their surname, so use this if you have reserved a restaurant or hotel eg Mein Name ist Herr/Frau Jones (my name is Jones)
- Whilst German is the main language in Switzerland, there will be some dialectic differences compared to Austria and Germany. These are mostly associated with greetings and farewells. Don't worry about them!

Language School
Sprachschule Julen
Bahnhofstrasse 19, +41 (0)27 967 7222, www.sprachschulejulen.ch.

Laundries and dry cleaners
Beat und Luisa Biner
Hofmattstrasse 2, Monday to Friday and Saturday morning, +41 (0)27 967 2987.
Laundry and dry cleaner.

Waschsalon Doli
Nicolina Viera, Chalet Arvenhof, Monday to Friday and Saturday morning, Hofmattstrasse 3, +41 (0)27 967 5100.

Womy-express Chem
Viktoria Center, +41 (0)27 967 3242.
Laundry and dry cleaner.

Left Luggage

You can leave your bags at Left Luggage or use the coin-operated lockers at the train station.

Lost Property (*Fundamt*)
Fundbüro

Haus Trifthorn, Am bach 7, Monday to Friday: 8-10am, 5-6pm, +41 (0)27 966 2222.

If you lose your ski pass, check at the nearest lift pass office to see if yours has been handed in. Always keep your receipt separately so you can get a new pass to replace it if it has not been found.

Massages

See page 125.

Money

All prices in this book are given in Swiss francs 'chf' unless the business is located on the Italian side of the ski area where prices are listed in euro (€).

At the time of going to press, the exchange rate was £1 for 2.4chf. You can find up-to-date exchange rates at www.xe.com.

For banks and cashpoints, see page 153.

Police (*Polizei*)
Cantonal police

Haus Cheminots B, Bahnhofplatz 3, Monday to Friday: 10am-12pm, 4-5.45pm, +41 (0)27 966 6920.

Community police

Haus Trifthorn, Am Bach 7, Monday to Friday: 8-10am, 5-6pm, +41 (0)27 966 2222.

Post office (*Postamt*)
Die Schweizerische Post

Turn right out of the station, when you reach UBS on the left you will see a pedestrian pathway through on the right; it's straight ahead, Monday to Friday: 8.30am-12pm, 1.45-6pm, Saturday: 8.30-11am.

You will see yellow post boxes dotted around the town. The one in the train station also has a stamp machine where you can buy stamps to the UK or you can get them from the postcard shops.

Public toilets

Found in the base lift stations, the train station and on the main street in Am Bach as well as in the major lift stations on the mountain.

Radio

Radio Rottu Oberwallis
+41 (0)27 948 0948.
97,8 MHz and 89,0 MHz on cable:
a news channel in different
languages providing information
about the Matter valley.

Road report

www.tcs.ch or call 163 from a
landline or Swiss mobile phone. +41
(0)848 800 163 from a UK mobile.

Dial +41 (0)27 967 4444 for
information on the condition of the
Täsch to Zermatt road if you're
planning to take a taxi rather than
the train.

Rubbish

Look out for the collection bins in
various places in the town
(including in the supermarkets) for
glass, batteries and cans. Even
stale bread can be recycled as
fodder for the local livestock –
dispose of it in the special sacks at
the refuse disposal points or on the
side of some *Stadels* (barns).

Safety

Ski resorts are usually a safe place
to holiday. Most crime involves theft
so ensure you keep your
belongings with you in the bar and
also keep your accommodation
locked at all times.

To protect your skis from theft,
you should get into the habit of
swapping skis with your companions
so you leave mismatched pairs (not
too close together) outside
restaurants and bars.

It is also worth knowing that
the local police aren't tolerant of
loud raucous behaviour on the way
home from bars and clubs at night.

Ski lockers

There are generally ski lockers in
every residence for your use, normally
with a security code to get in.

If your accommodation is
some way from the lifts, or you
have children with you, it might be
easier to use the public ski lockers
at the bottom of the main lift
stations (Gornergrat, Sunnegga
Express, Matterhorn Express) and
in the train station.

Alternatively you may be able
to store gear with your hire shop.

Taxis

In resort:
Taxi Zermatt
+41 (0)848 11 12 12
Recently amalgamated taxi service made up of four electro taxi services with a GPS system to reduce waiting times. Taxis cost around 15chf depending on the length of your journey and you can share costs with other people going the same way if there aren't many of you.

Between Täsch and Zermatt:
Many of these taxi services will offer a discounted rate for parking your car with them as well as taking their taxi to Zermatt.

Alphubel Taxi Parking
Täsch, +41 (0)27 967 1550, www.alphubel.ch.

Taxi Christophe
Leander Imesch, Täsch, +41 (0)27 967 3535, www.taxichristophe.ch. 24 hour.

Taxi Eden/Taxi Metro
Familie Mathieu Monteiro, Täsch, +41 (0)27 967 6444, www.taxi-metro.com. 24 hour.

Taxi Elite
Johann Imesch, Hotel Elite, Täsch, +41 (0)27 967 1226, hotel.elite.taesch@bluewin.ch.

Taxi Fredy

Fredy Arnold, Täsch, +41 (0)27 967 3366, www.taxifredy.ch. 24 hour.

Taxi Schaller
Max Schaller, Täsch, +41 (0)27 967 1212, www.taxischaller.com.

Telephones
There are public telephones throughout Zermatt in places such as the train station and the post office. For more information, see page 4.

Time
Swiss time is GMT +1 hour.

Tipping

Restaurants and bars: Because there is normally a service charge included in your bill, the Swiss don't really tip other than to round up. However, if you have had special service or food, leave a few extra francs.

Instructors: There are no set rules for tipping instructors, some people do and some people don't. It's up to the individual but if you've had a great lesson, then it's a nice gesture to tip them 15-20chf.

Chalet hosts: Most survive the season on next to nothing so if your host makes a positive difference to your holiday, they will not be offended by a cash gift at the end of the week! If you had good service, you should tip at least 15-20chf per guest

Tourist office
Zermatt Tourismus

Bahnhofplatz 5, Monday to Saturday: 8.30am-12pm, 1.30-6pm, Sunday: 9.30am-12pm, 4-6pm, +41 (0)27 966 8100, www.zermatt.ch.

The staff in the tourist office in Zermatt are all very helpful. You can pick up village maps from their office as well as getting advice on most things.

The office has an electronic board where you can check out the locations of hotels, B&Bs and apartments, and call the owners to check availability. The tourist office website also has information about the town's accommodation options.

Trains

There are two types of train in Zermatt; the Matterhorn Gotthard Railway which brings you to Zermatt from Brig, Visp or Täsch, and the Gornergrat Bahn which takes you from Zermatt up onto the Gornergrat mountain:

Matterhorn Gotthard Railway

+41 (0)27 927 7777, www.mgbahn.ch.

For more information, see page 18. For the Glacier Express, see page 133.

Gornergrat Bahn

Bahnhofplatz, +41 (0)27 921 4111, www.gornergrat.ch. Departing approximately every twenty minutes from Zermatt, this rack-and-pinion railway is one of the most scenic journeys you take. With new twin-level entry cars, the service looks like it will become more comfortable and maybe even faster – it currently takes about 40 minutes to wind its way to the top of Gornergrat. Get out and investigate the various stops along the way or use the train as skiing transport.

Zermatt Bergbahnen AG

+41 (0)27 966 0101, www.matterhornparadise.ch.

The Zermatt lift company - Mountain Cableways - with information on lifts, prices and times.

Weather

Weather report: 162 or +41 (0)848 800 162

It's difficult to predict the weather for Zermatt as it is surrounded by so many huge mountains that its microclimate often produces totally different weather to the adjacent resorts. It can get seriously cold in January (-25°C) and the Klein Matterhorn (glacier) side is always colder than the Sunnegga side. The most important thing is to prepare for everything when packing for your trip.

Zermatt's glacier is open all year round, but the main lift system opens in late November/early December and shuts at the end of April or beginning of May. In November on the glacier, there is normally a decent covering with some early powder days. At the end of season, the snow is usually fantastic and the glacier means you can ski good snow all day.

The following provide current weather forecasts:

maddogski.com – current weather forecasts, snow reports and webcams
www.snow-forecast.com – three day weather forecasts or six day forecasts for members
www.meteoswiss.ch – a Swiss weather website that provides details on how heavily it is snowing in various regions and how that will affect transport
www.zermatt.ch – Zermatt tourist office's website with the current weather on the homepage

Index

And finally...

We would like to thank the following people for their help and support: Susie Aust, Peter Beaty, Philip Blackwell, Carrie Hainge at the Ski Club of Great Britain, Reuben Goddard, Paul Hammett, Iain Hardcastle, Pauline Imboden, Jenny Jones, Karin Schmid, Jessica Schwab, the Zermatt Tourist office, Janelle Stettler, Carrie Stokes, Nadine Stothard, Helen Taylor, Nikk Vaughan.

Photo credits

Ariadna de Raadt – P122
Christiania Hotel – P134
Carmen Martínez – P91
Christof-Sonderegger, Zermatt Tourism – P81
Colin Soutar – P114
Ed Ward – P14
Gaby de Pace – P86, 88, 96, 128
Harald Fischer – P68
Henry Meredith Hardy – P41, 47
Dividers: About Mad Dog, On the piste, Other things to do
Kate Whittaker – P7, 10, 11, 17, 89, 107, 131, 136, 137
Divider: The List

Kurt Mueller, Zermatt Tourism – P20
Divider – About Zermatt, Planning your trip
Oliver Lee – P2, 6, 31, 38, 58, 63, 74, 101
Oliver Ritz, Zermatt Tourism – P45, 76, 94, 96, 109, 111, 112, 117, 124, 142, 144, 152
Divider: Food and drink, Children
Popov Maxim – P42
Yanik Chauvin – P126
Zermatt Bergbahnen, Zermatt Tourism – P23, 28

Do you know something we don't? Jot down your tips and recommendations and let us know about them at info@maddogski.com

_____

_____

_____

_____

_____

_____

_____